Meet Divine Mother

An Intimate Introduction
to
the Other Half of Heaven

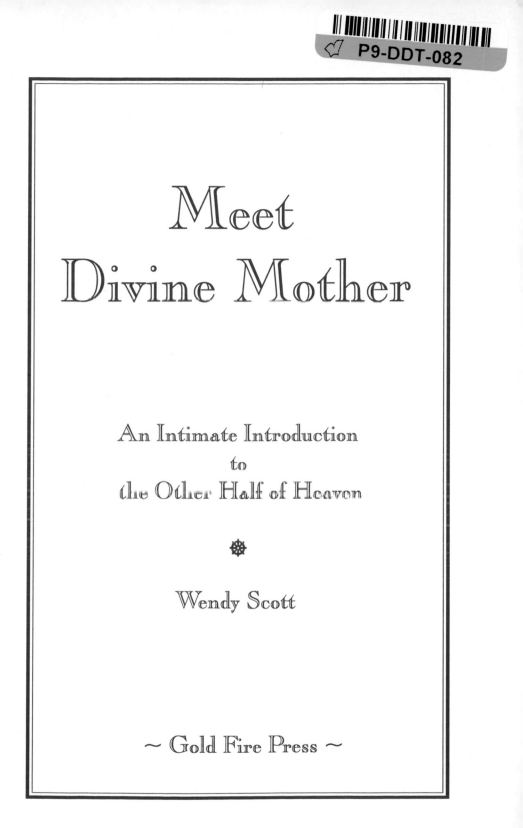

Wendy Scott

~ Gold Fire Press ~

ISBN: 1-893724-00-X

Library of Congress Catalogue Number: 99-71504

Printed in the United States of America
Publishers Press
Salt Lake City, Utah

First Edition

GOLD FIRE PRESS
P. O. Box 12873
Marina del Rey, California
90295

To the only sun, moon and star,
who know who they are;
And to my beloved DPW, sister of my heart
and companion in faith.

❀

Acknowledgements

The unseen angels:
Edna Johnson, whose prayers and faith made a difference; Diane Johnson Stewart who, along with her mother, remembers my "imaginary friend" in childhood; Arthur Small and Marian Small who stood strong for what they had not yet seen manifest; HL who stood her ground; LH who stands alone in love; DPW and DM who stand together in light; TSM and CNM who stand out in my heart and in the world; Sara Sakuma who stands for fine work; John Frank Rosenblum who stands ready to help; and "all you other Folks" who stand fast with impeccable guidance, and always have.

❀

Photography Credits

p. 8, Personal archives
Inserts:
1) Courtesy of Jeff Williams, photographer/Media Photo 2) Personal archives 3) Courtesy of Longfellow's Wayside Inn 4) Jim Proodian, photographer 5) Courtesy of the National Park Service, Longfellow National Historic Site 6) Courtesy of the National Park Service, Longfellow National Historic Site 7) Courtesy of the National Park Service, Longfellow National Historic Site 8) Personal archives, KCRA Sacramento 9) Courtesy of the National Park Service, Longfellow National Historic Site 10) Personal archives, KCRA Sacramento 11) Bust, courtesy of the National Park Service, Longfellow National Historic Site. Suite of photographs on right: (a) Personal archives (b) Personal archives, KCRA Sacramento (c) Personal archives (d) Photographer courtesy of the Hart Agency, Boston 12) The two photographs above, personal archives; the two photographs below, courtesy of the National Park Service, Longfellow National Historic Site 13) Els Knoppers, photographer

CONTENTS

Connecting...

"For the rest of my life
I want to reflect on what light is."

Albert Einstein

To the Reader

Dear One~

Astonishingly, there is no account of Divine Mother by anyone in the West who knows Her. Books on the Cosmic Mother and pagan Goddess exist, but they are grounded in ancient, primitive beliefs about a female deity none of us has met and, from the sound of it, might not want to. That material does not rise from earth-bound mythology or supposition to encompass the all-embracing Reality of light, love, truth and intelligence that is Divine Mother, nor does it explain how to meet Her here and now.

This book does.

Based on a life-long metaphysical and spiritual relationship with Divine Mother, it uniquely details exactly who She is and how you can meet Her today in Divine Meditation where She appears as a beautiful woman willing to resolve our concerns; facilitate personal transformation in the light; lovingly reveal, unravel and correct our individual karma, and release us into the infinite joy and freedom of Being that is our birthright as Her children.

Meet Divine Mother charts the precise route to these ends and more, making it a concrete bridge to higher consciousness and enlightenment. Each page is a step dedicated to leading you into a private relationship with the one long missing from our awareness of spiritual and cosmic Reality: the other half of heaven, Divine Mother God.

What you will read took five decades to experience, understand and then write with a tenacity for accuracy. Only a few names have been changed in what is, as it was meant to be, a heartfelt gift from Divine Mother *to you*. When followed, it guarantees a life of love, joy, freedom and light.

Wendy Scott
Los Angeles, California, 1999

1

Divine Mother

Divine Mother is our co-creator. She is the other half of heaven and as real as the air we breathe. Meeting Her face to face is only a meditation away.

Those statements are not assumptions based on Her alleged existence in the past. They are the result of *experiencing Divine Mother here and now* in a relationship so compelling and enlightening over the course of a lifetime that it became impossible not to share with you who She is, how She transforms our lives and how you can meet Her, too.

Divine Mother has referred to these pages as the trail of a mystic, a paper pathway leading you directly back to Her and therefore back to the equilibrium of spiritual balance that was our uninterrupted Reality long ago.

To make sure the trail is easier to follow than it was to forge, however, we will occasionally stop on our chronological journey, make camp and sit by the fire for true tales of the mistakes I made while traversing the wilderness long impeding access to Her. Taking a little after Lewis and Clark, who only had to go the wrong way once so no one else would have to do it again, every hazard is mapped in red. By sidestepping each one, you can follow a corrected path without ever wondering why it is correct and, by book's end, walk confidently into a relationship with Her of your own.

Since that is the case, and since all the stories of my trip, the ups and the downs, are teaching tools approved by Divine Mother to make certain your way, She and I will periodically come to you on these pages hand in hand.

But there is another reason for the pairing.

Long ago, we each could say, "I know Divine Mother. I know She is the mother of my soul. I know She is the light, truth and intelligence in the universe. Since I am part of the universe, I know She is in me as well." We knew that these powerful, permanent connections to Her were unassailable aspects of Reality; that they are irrevocably linked to us like a spiritual form of DNA, and that Her influence cannot be separated from anyone. Because this is eternally true, no one has an accurate account of Divine Mother if it does not include Her effect in their life, just as no one has a complete knowledge of Reality if She is not known.

For that reason, both Divine Mother and Reality will come to you hand in hand on these pages too, often dramatically so, from perceiving Her presence in childhood to prophetic dreams, unerring telepathy and confirmable revelations in adulthood. There were disastrous years in between, as you will see, when awareness of Divine Mother was lost or not embraced until She undeniably revealed Herself to be *the maternal source and visual voice of knowledge and Reality*.

Like the combination of light, truth and intelligence, knowledge and Reality can be received from Divine Mother just by talking to Her. A cozy chat may seem difficult now, but continuous communication with Her was once as free-flowing as water. Nothing obstructed that right early on and nothing obstructs it today.

The *illusion* of difficulty, however, does exist and it took a particularly pernicious hold on our minds around the time of Christ. That is when the patriarchy in the West, but also in the East, was allowed to usurp religious and therefore political power over humanity by denying the Reality of Divine Mother. Unbelievably, the West even went so far as to supplant Her in oral and written tradition with an innocent bystander, Mary, who had never put in for a promotion; she didn't need one. Once that was done, however, it was only a matter of time before Divine Mother could be neatly decapitated from the Godhead in favor of the Father without anyone much the wiser. Out of sight, out of mind.

To stave off the possibility She might somehow still be remembered, Divine Mother was deleted in other ways. In Christianity, for example, the Trinity became universally known as "Father, Son and Holy Ghost" instead of the original and natural "Father, *Mother* and Son." Even Buddhism, despite the repeated admonition of the Buddha never to forget Her, dismissed Divine Mother as an inner wisdom virtually impossible to achieve, rather than revering Her as the very means by which to attain it.

In truth, Divine Mother cannot be deleted from any mind in any way. Yet to maintain the patriarchy, Her authority and autonomy continued to be distorted, discredited and denied throughout entire continents and down through the ages by many misnomers: the pagan Goddess, Mother Nature, Mother Earth, a myth, a feminine principle, a channeled entity, a figment of the imagination.

In time, apart from folklore and an occasional fairy tale, the only traces of Divine Mother's existence were generally found in the primitive cave drawings of distant lands or in ancient artifacts depicting Her image in form. As the sole surviving clues of Her whereabouts, these comparative trinkets consistently pointed in the wrong direction. Rather than taking us into ourselves to find Her, they led us into the earth; we became excavators and archeologists, tillers of the soil instead of the soul.

The radical deviation from the spiritual to the physical which occurred when Divine Mother was amputated from awareness did not make us angry; it made us the walking wounded. We accepted the loss of an entire God parent as a matter of course, trying to traverse through life and the centuries on one leg as it were, when any stable progress, personal or global, requires the balance of two.

In our stumbling attempts to move forward, we went backwards, tripping over questions whose answers had once been common knowledge: Who am I and why am I here? Where did I come from and where am I going? The only reason we are still without answers at this late date is because we have not had access to the one who knows them: Divine Mother.

But we do have the opportunity now, as well as the responsibility, to rectify the profound errors of the past and regain what was lost. We can all meet Divine Mother again in Divine Meditation, the telepathic and visual form of inner communication detailed in this book where She appears as a beautiful woman more than willing to talk with us.

When we take the time to meet Divine Mother within ourselves, we realize that having forgotten Her does not mean She has ever forgotten us. Instead, She has been waiting all along with open arms, ready to offer the riches held in readiness for our return. These blessings are so valid and right, so perfectly in step with what we need and desire, that we understand by direct experience what cannot ever be denied: Divine Mother is present and alive, eager to fulfill Her position as Mother God in front of our eyes, travel with us on the journey of life and, mercifully, explain everything as we go.

She is an indomitable and infallible companion who greets us with encouragement, protects us at every turn, and meets all our soul-mothering needs with wisdom, grace and humor. It is Her pleasure to comfort and guide us, to make clear our way by knowing in advance what lies on the road ahead—and exactly how to handle it. As we travel on, whatever we ask is answered because *if it concerns us, it is of concern to Her*.

Divine Mother so perfectly understands our personal psychology, and our receptivity to important information, that *She always knows what to say, when to say it and how to say it in ways each of us can and will hear*. This is true as well for the content of past lives when they are revealed in words or run on the screen of our mind like movies for our review. Once a lifetime is understood and corrected, any potential negative karma from it naturally dissolves. Fear vanishes, peace takes its place, love gains momentum, and our purpose on the planet is not just made clear, it is made manifest. Even happiness, that elusive fellow forever on the run, is captured by Divine Mother and permanently detained in our hearts.

And then, just when we think there can't possibly be more, Divine Mother leads us to an unexpected destination, one made inevitable from first meeting Her again: the grace of enlightenment, our journey's natural end.

That is when we can see that our life, which so often had appeared like a maze in the darkness, is really the amazing story of Her light in us all—joyously illuminating our true identity as Her children, beloved Beings of light.

As you will read later, the end result of Her light, my light, or anyone else's light was extremely difficult to fathom when I was very ill and tormented by my own ignorance:

Why am I sick? Where is God? Where is the truth? Why aren't my prayers answered? Why am I so afraid, confused and angry? Where did this guilt come from? What is wrong with me? Why is my personal karma overwhelming? Why is it so hard to understand anything when I know in my heart that I came here to understand everything?

Divine Mother's question to me then, and ultimately to each one of us, was very unexpected: "What if all the terrible things you ever thought about yourself weren't true?"

Hope flickered in the prospect, but just as easily extinguished. I didn't have the advantage then of knowing She is real. There was no book in my hands, as there is one now in yours, to say "She is telling you the truth." As much as I listened to Her in the early days of Divine Meditation, I didn't yet have enough external confirmation of what She said to take Her word on faith alone.

In reponse to my mounting doubt, Divine Mother created this scene in meditation, not once but many times:

I was in a great room at night. To the west, a wall of floor-to-ceiling windows overlooked the beach and the ocean beyond. Gunfire and bombs exploded loudly on the sand and lit up the dark night sky. A terrible battle was being waged there and it was of great concern to me.

In contrast to this chaos, the interior of the room was tranquil, warm, inviting. Divine Mother sat in a large, comfortable chair next to a fire in the fireplace. Her position at the north end of the room was like the arrow of a compass by which to gauge one's direction.

She told me telepathically that the war outside was illusion: I had projected the battle I waged within myself onto the beach, but it was not any more real than the perception of myself as unhappy, inadequate and ill.

Divine Mother then turned my attention to the east wall. I could see that it was entirely lined with mirrors. She told me to look in them to see who I really am.

Still young at these internal endeavors, very fearful and fresh from the raging battle, I was hardly in the mood to see a vision of myself ravaged by war. It took a long time to find the courage to look in the mirror.

I started low, with the reflection of my feet, and my eyes widened to find them shoed not in combat boots, but in burgundy velvet slippers. As my gaze slowly traveled upward, I saw myself clothed in a full-length burgundy gown from the Renaissance. The collar was trimmed with white lace, my figure slim and elegant.

I stood on a hillside in the country and the grass grew in green, healthy waves beneath my feet. The sun shone strongly and peace pervaded the scene. At last I dared look up at my face: it was just beautiful, so radiant and happy, so free of concern.

Divine Mother said softly,, "This, my dear girl, is Joy. This is who you really are."

Undone by the illness, overweight, deeply depressed, without loved ones near or a job in the offing, this was an incongruity to say the least. Having seen myself as Ms. Misery for so long, Divine Mother's pronouncement was simply astounding and, from where I stood then, scarcely worthy of credence.

What is far more astounding, however, is that it absolutely came to pass. As you will later see in detail, there was a profound inner "renaissance" with Divine Mother in the form of a spiritual rebirth—into Joy. The interaction with Divine Mother in Divine Meditation brought about the removal of everything other than light until only Joy remained. The warring conflict ceased, answers replaced questions, and for the first time in my life I had the freedom to be, to be who I really am.

The power inherent in that renewal, coupled with Divine Mother having perfectly and graphically illustrated it beforehand, invoked unconditional faith in Her. I just could not understand until it happened that one of the results of the luminous alchemy occurring for anyone in a sustained relationship with Divine Mother is the manifestation of the True Self: Joy.

To participate in such life-altering communion with Her requires only reunion with Her. When that is achieved, you too will know that Divine Mother is the other half of heaven, the missing link in our spiritual heritage and parentage who instructs and informs us, enlightens and transforms us, comforts and supports us, loves and transports us, encourages and adores us. She is the real lantern in the darkness, the beacon illuminating our creation as Beings of light and pointing out the path of liberation from all the problems of this world, the True Mother every soul seeks and can find again, here and now.

The next chapter explains how I first knew all of these things about Her are true—and how what was so naturally known in childhood could have been so unnaturally lost.

The author at three.

2

In the Beginning

Along with my mother and both grandparents, Divine Mother was part of my earliest childhood. It was as normal for me to sit on the couch and have conversations with Her as it was to stand on a stool and help Grandma stir cake batter in a mixing bowl. At the ages of three and four, it wouldn't have entered my mind to question the reality of Divine Mother talking with me in the living room any more than I would have questioned the reality of Grandma baking cakes in the kitchen.

The adults, however, did question my relationship with someone they could not see or hear. Their concern was evident as they paced up and down our little two-bedroom home in San Gabriel, shaking their heads. My openly referring to Divine Mother as "Madre," which means Mother in Spanish, only made them pick up the pace. Like the whole town then, we were of Anglo-Saxon, not Hispanic, descent.

The house had been built in 1948, the year of my birth and the year we moved in, on land honored for thousands of years by its original inhabitants, the Gabrielino Indians. If my family or any of the neighbors in their own new houses on the same new street had known that the Gabrielinos were one with all that is Divine, any number of them might have had an inkling as to the identity of Madre—but no one did. So instead of accurately defining Her as Mother God, my family pounced on a plausible alternative in a book my mother was reading by a fellow named Spock. Grandpa paused mid-pace at the prospect and Grandma smiled in relief as my mother concluded in accordance with the parental Bible of its time, "Oh, Madre must be an imaginary friend!"

They were very proud to have "solved" the mystery so easily, but I knew She wasn't made up. I knew She was the Real Mother, albeit I had no idea at the time what that meant. This wonderful Woman was simply a given in the reality that was mine as a child, and what a reality it was.

A Personal Eden

The land once held sacred by the Gabrielino Indians had become part of the San Gabriel Mission less than a mile away, nurtured later as a walnut grove, and then turned into the spectacular expanse of—my own backyard.

More than two lots long, Grandpa had fashioned a series of gardens connected by concrete stepping-stones. In one, morning dew glistened on deep-green leaves and pretty pink flowers could be made to open their mouths and then snap like a dragon. Lanky gladiolus waved in the wind, not far from where the tiny mosses lived. Ferns flourished in a dell by the elm, a towering neighbor for an arbor of grapes growing green on the vine. Yellow hibiscus preened along a far wall in brazen contrast to the delicate cherry blossoms, daisies and graceful columbine.

In another garden, vanilla-cream roses, heady with their own scent, luxuriated in the afteroon heat. Burly avocado and walnut trees, rooted in a protective stance, kindly stretched out their leafy limbs to shield Grandma's rhubarb and Grandpa's strawberries from the blazing sun, dappling the dusty earth with shade. The purple San Gabriel Mountains beckoned as close as a mother's breasts, and the California air sparkled, the sky a blue only God had made.

In the early evening, Grandma would switch on the

porch light and let me run in the grass that Grandpa had cut but not yet raked, and dance in the blades with my shadow. At night, resting against a feather pillow and bedded in between clean cotton sheets that smelled like the sun because Grandma dried them outside on the line, I would fall asleep to the rhythm of crickets coming in through the open window, content in the peace created by everything combined.

In the harmony of color and sound, in the light and life all around, there existed only the profound security of truth. The beautiful Woman with me, who talked to me and guided me, in the house and in the gardens, was so connected to this, and I to Her, there was no need to speak.

My mother did not understand my silence as the inaudible sound of appreciation and regarded me as nearly autistic. It wasn't autism, or even always appreciation; it was self protection: with Dr. Spock's baby book out in the open, and my mother's tendency to misapply it, this was hardly a safe house for the divinely attuned.

Within a very short time, for example, the self-containment and independence that mark a relationship with Divine Mother were misread by my mother as a rejection of her as a parent. Even the curious pink spot between my eyebrows was mislabeled a birthmark when it was, as it is, the active third eye of inner sight allowing visual access to Divine Mother and all of Reality. Everyone has a third eye, but it is wide open in those so very young. This is why, I believe, Christ said we must become like little children to enter the kingdom of heaven—we must be able to see truth again as we did then.

At the other end of the scale, my grandparents were captivated by my devotion to an "imaginary friend." Grandpa would ask, "So, how is Madre today?" I would look over at Divine Mother sitting quietly on the couch, turn back to him and report, "Fine." He would then dramatically side-step where I had just looked and whisper, "Don't want to trip over Her."

I'd just say, "Oh, good. She doesn't want you to trip

over Her, either," and go back to counting buttons. Grandma had a big box of them that proved to be an endless fascination, they were so colorful and shiny. I didn't know until many years later that they symbolize protection and I had really been counting my blessings.

Grandma might then suggest that Madre and I play with my dolls in the bedroom, and along She would come in these very early attempts at mothering, guiding the diaper changes and the baby baths, the hugging and the holding. A stroll with perfectly powdered and sweet-smelling babies followed in their carriage on the walk in front of the house where the pansies grew. If anyone had looked, they would have noticed a little girl pushing her dolls along in the sunlight; but anyone using inner sight would have seen a little girl walking with Divine Mother. None of us is ever alone.

Later, as an adult, I wondered how I knew to name Divine Mother "Madre," it was so perfect. Either this was a child's way of trying to conceal Her true identity from the non-believers in the house while still being accurate, or She had told me. It was probably both, but it also turned out to be so much more:

A few years ago, and to my utter astonishment, a television documentary on India, the oldest civilization in the world, included a town in which only Divine Mother is worshiped. I can't spell for you the name of that town, I never saw it, but I heard it pronounced as clear as a bell: *Madre.*

The Serpent

My private Eden stopped dead the day sexual abuse entered this perfection, almost shattering it entirely and me along with it around the age of three and-a-half and four. Such unfathomable betrayal precipitated a mind-split, a wrenching from Reality, during the very instant in which I couldn't trust the one human being with whom I had been linked on this earth even by a physical umbilicus—my own mother.

To cope with the overwhelming trauma of maternal sexual abuse, and in instant defiance of it, a false self, the ego, erupted into existence. I *felt* it happen. And I believed its promise of protection: we would expand the false self in order to shield the true self, the Golden Girl of light within, that lovely child in the gardens communing daily with Divine Mother, and in that way, you see, we would save her.

But that's not what happened. Instead of safeguarding me against harm from my mother, the ego took a stand between me and Divine Mother. Somehow I had inadvertently made a pact with the devil and couldn't quite remember to reach out for Her or return my allegiance to the truth and light and beauty all around. That made it a double coup for evil, then; it had master-minded the loss of two mothers.

This was a classic demonstration of the birth of the ego, its intimate camaraderie as insidious as a snake, seducing my mind into following it off God's path, down a dead end trail of hurt, anger, self-deprecation and, far too often, self-erasure. It was, too, so analogous to the Garden of Eden: purity and innocence lost through the mistaken choice of listening to the lying voice of a snaking ego instead of the knowing voice of a loving God.

For a time after we have entered this world from the other side, we continue to know the unalterable truth of Reality. Everything is one in the light; there is no separation and no darkness to fear. Yet something happens to each one of us, individually, to establish the ego and furnish its domain, the negative mind. It may be incest, a move, abuse, the death of a parent, the birth of a sibling, arguments overheard, an illness—anything that is different from the unity we have known. The event is perceived as disruptive to what has otherwise been uninterrupted truth. Without effective coping skills, we personalize what has occurred apart from ourselves and then make the mistake of separating with it. We no longer identify with the Divine but with the intruding event and begin moving away from God.

That is the generalization of what occurs. When it

comes to specifics, no one, not even psychoanalysts, know the precise way such an event enters our particular psyche, the exact and erratic route it travels into our assumptions about the world and ourselves, or its explicit effect in the mind. If they could, none of us would be suffering now. Instead, trauma requires both our maturation for evaluation and the conscious reconnection with God to restore awareness of the original unity. There is a reason for these requirements, and another reason the ego exists at all, but we are not at that point in our story yet.

We are at the point just now where my story is your story, too. We all have a Golden Child of God within, and an ego developed from a sense of separation. As a result, every one of us experiences conflict between what the Golden Child knows and what the ego mind thinks. Most people don't transcend this duality, or understand that the personality contradictions it creates stem *only* from accepting the false thinking of the ego instead of the true knowing of God.

Once in existence, the ego set me, as it does all of us, abruptly adrift in the illusion of life, my only traveling companion it seemed, not Divine Mother, but this scaly, limbless reptile. Since nothing felt normal from the inception of the ego on, its constant and cryptic counsel not to talk at all now, "Don't tell," appeared very wise, especially when my mother remarried just as I turned seven.

To entice me to join the new family, she advertised it as an opportunity for a new home, a new school, and a new life on a new land several miles away in Arcadia, but to me that was the horror. It would mean being left to my own resources, the only person who knew this woman wasn't sane, and it would mean abandoning the sole stability in sight— my grandparents, and the now unconscious remembrance of Divine Mother waiting quietly for me in the gardens.

I refused to go for over a year, so clear was the inner knowledge that certain doom lay ahead. When my baby brother was born, the pressure increased to complete the "storybook" family. I went then without a choice, but on one unspoken condition to my mother, as clear in my mind today as it was then: "You can take me, but you can't take all of me."

I hid the precious part for safety, tucking the Golden Girl of the garden even deeper within, and, on the ego's advice, searched for the protection of a competent facade. The choices available in 1956, however, were far from endless. Television news offered the likes of Mamie Eisenhower or Mamie Van Doren, such extremes that I was forced to select a role model closer to home: Grandma. When that proved too old for even the most mature of third-graders, I reached into my grab bag of private personality options and pulled up an unexpected stash of self-confidence. Where on earth such poise had come from I did not know then, but it did the job; I seemed as intact as ever.

Now *how* I was going to get out of the false and back to the true didn't enter my head, nor had that snake of an ego included any instructions. But I certainly could tell by the way it slithered along pointlessly in the sand, with all the get-up-and-go of a slug, that finding the path back to Eden and Divine Mother would be a long time a-comin', Lord, a long time.

Twenty-four years to be exact, and this is why:

The dread of being with my mother proved prophetic, so there was not much time to cast off a persona. Instead, and much worse, it stuck to me like a second skin during my mother's subsequent nervous breakdowns, alcoholic binges, near catatonic depressions, shock treatments, prescription drugs, suicide attempts, and psychiatric hospitalizations. I became the housekeeper, the care-taker, my little brother's only mother.

Any remaining reality came crashing down when my otherwise responsible stepfather, an aeronautical engineer, found working in a wind tunnel and later on the space shuttle far easier than dealing with my mother. There was a period when he would vanish for days at a time and I, at 15, was left alone with her ... the trail of blood from the slit wrists, the near-overdoses, the suburban neighbors gathering to gossip on their front lawns whenever she was taken away. Yet who could blame him for wanting to disappear? My mother went to bars alone; spiralled head first through the windshield after crashing drunk into another car on Christmas Eve; put an icepick to her chest, leaned against the bureau to drive it into her heart, but missed; and once she tried to gas herself in the garage. My stepfather was home that time, watching television. I heard the car running, raced outside, found the garage door locked and saw through the window my mother slumped over the steering wheel. After the ambulance left with assurances she would be all right, and that finding her had saved her life, I returned to the car in prayer for her—and discovered a note she had written to my grandmother: "Please take care of Peter," my little brother.

There was no mention of me.

Her deeply hurtful disregard for my welfare, shown so many different ways over the years, crystallized that night. It seemed a devastating part of her illness and my own inadequacy as a human being, only because I hadn't recalled the sexual abuse. It wasn't possible to know she regarded me as a time-bomb of submerged memory to be denied at all cost, especially when my single concern was to suppress my needs and help her. I fully believed that the dual carte blanche of "mentally ill" and "mother" meant there was every reason to forgive her no matter how she treated me, even after she got better. And from 1964 on, she simply cast my fate to the wind, although it felt more like a windstorm when money ran out to support her private psychiatric hospitalizations that year and she was committed to Norwalk State Mental Hospital for a condition that never had a name.

Often no one was home then. I desperately needed grounding, but the windstorm quickly turned into a sandstorm: straight A's since the fifth grade tumbled and I unexpectedly lost a school election. There wasn't time to recover before the earthquake struck: my boyfriend, whom I adored, suddenly and catastrophically decided to leave me. I thought his unrelenting verbal cruelty to ensure that end had come about because my family situation was so damning, and I worthless because of it, but he explained years later that it was an uncommunicated and poorly executed kindness: we had been on the verge of making love for the first time and he hadn't want me to become pregnant.

Not understanding he had substituted cruelty for a condom, so many losses coming one after another were over-whelming. The only way I could even hope to cope was to put the false self in motion, a poised smile in place to cover the pain. The Golden Girl could stand behind this increasingly fragile facade and, please God, survive.

Still, despite all odds, I *did* find God in this period, or at least the notion of God. There was an epiphany one night at the beach as I wandered along the water's edge and watched the waves come crashing on shore with the same rhythm and intensity as the disasters hitting my life. But I couldn't help notice, too, that the waves were visibly white in the darkness, beautiful in their own way, and always con-cluded in calm—in a pale, moonlit froth that bubbled into the wet sand and disappeared. There was no lasting effect of the waves on the shore.

I had no idea this was a gimpse far into my future when Divine Mother would prove to me beyond a shadow of a doubt that, like the inability of the waves to affect the shore, nothing in life can affect the innate integrity of the soul. I only knew then the cataclysmic joy of having faith in the power behind the calm: God was the way to keep body and soul together while others were losing theirs.

It was faith like this that enabled me to write the fol-lowing letter to my grandfather, copied here verbatim, when I was 15. He had been diagnosed with colon cancer, and the letter—kept by his bedside for years in its original enve-lope and returned to me after he died—was written in sup-port of his attempts to bolster the belief in God he always felt had been inadequate but desperately needed to survive the pain of living and the uncertainties of death.

February 27, 1964

Hello Sweetheart,

How are you feeling? I'm so mad at myself for not calling you or doing something for you, but darn, I've got stupid problems, too.

I get wrapped up in my own worries but when I think of the problems so much deeper and more important that others must bear, my depressions subside, I resolve to help others, and God seems so near.

I have never felt as close to God as I do now. The discovery of God and faith, through prayer, is so beautiful. He is a friend; someone to love and turn to when the world seems like Hell, and then He is there to give you the love He's been offering right along. With this realization, faith and guidance are there for the asking, for these are unselfish requests and are answered in their utterance.

"For when a man can leave himself and enter the lives of others, he leaves his own heart open so that God may enter and dwell with him."

I'm sure this has happened to you, you are so strong, and I know you believe. This is the way it should be, and really, since there is a God, the only feelings we could have for life.

I love you and pray for you, Grandpa.

Wendy

3

The Other Shoe Drops

It would be nice to say the next cartload of unpleasantness was delivered to the wrong door, but it definitely came addressed to me and, like everything else in this book, really happened. Along with events in the prior chapter, it will be used later to illustrate how deftly Divine Mother dissolves our misfortune, no matter how much or what kind, once we have a conscious relationship with Her again.

At 16, and presumably to protect me from the circumstances in California, I was sent to France to live with someone I did not know: my American father. He had left before I was born, but his parting words to my mother, with all the drama of a dime-store novel, echoed long after his departure, "I have more to give the world than a wife and child."

I can just see him throwing a cape over one shoulder, his arm extended out gallantly as he prepared to charge off into the great unknown, his young wife on her knees, round of belly, tugging at the edge of his cape, begging him to stay, but, "Nay, woman! I have more to give the world than a wife and child."

I never did find out whose idea it was to send me to this man, particularly when my mother was committed to a mental institution for completely different reasons. All I knew was that it seemed as if a French version of the Bronte sisters had suddenly picked up the potboiler's pen and written the next searing scenes of my life in the dead of night, because I was certainly about to live in a different century— and a very dark one.

My father had achieved enough success in the years since the disappearing cape to warrant in his own mind the acquisition of a new wife and three other children, but only my stepmother knew about me; my father did not inform the "little ones" of my existence until the night before my arrival. It was an ominous sign of things to come, because once I was actually there, so far from home, without friends, support, or a language to call my own, it became very apparent that I was not only an inconvenience, but, as he told my new half-brother, "a mistake."

Nonetheless, I was instructed to say that I loved him each night before going to bed, even though he would not offer the same in return. It was only at my insistence that he finally did, and of course the sentiment did not ring true to ears which had listened for the same-sought sincerity from my mother for years. It was unfathomable to me that both parents, 6,000 miles and 16 years apart, could possibly have the same disaffected attitude toward their own daughter. When I dared confront him and my stepmother about the lack of love, he actually said, "We can't love you. You never offered us the joys of a child."

I took the fall for that, because it was true, I hadn't. It bothered me greatly until I thought, "What is wrong with this picture?" Oh, yes. They were *gone* during my childhood.

My father had spent those years at UC Berkeley, and then at the University of Chicago School of Law becoming an international lawyer. It was the most honorable profession because, to him, it demanded respect. I don't think he could have been respected otherwise, not when he had to be constantly admired for *his* intelligence and *his* interests, not to mention the sacrifices *he* and *his* family had to endure simply because I, this black sheep, this now non-member of any family, was there.

My father extended an invitation to become part of the family, but as a black sheep confronted by that kind of ego, it was a little hard to fit in. Besides, he reveled in mind games that mentally offered a seat but took the chair away, and he played them as if it were an equal competition in which his victory over a 16-year-old actually counted.

That pushed me away, but no one was allowed close. My father had few friends and, I later learned, not even those liked him. It took time to unlock what was so wrong with him but eventually one key fit perfectly: he wasn't genuine. By relying on his ego instead of an authentic sense of self, character for him was still something that could be lifted from a book and worn as easily as one of those capes.

He had raised his sights over the years from the dimestore variety to the 18th century "Age of Reason," however, donning the mental garb of the morally upright as his own. The man reeked of righteousness and ran the roost from a patriarchal perch he had poached from literary figures of the period. He quoted his pedantic mentors with the less than subtle hint that my upbringing lacked an equivalent "moral fiber." Since my poor grades over the last few months in California also spoke volumes to him about either a questionable mental capacity or how I didn't try, he thought I should come to know the masters, too.

The only Master I wanted to know was Jesus, but according to my father, He hadn't lived in the right century.

We visited a monastery that spring, not for the religious value, but for a concert of 18th-century chamber music, something my mother hadn't quite had time to introduce between breakdowns. My father viewed this lack of exposure as a failing on my part, and I was made to feel as if an essential ingredient in the composition of a decent human being had been irretrievably lost—particularly when he punished me for listening to Joan Baez, or even the Hermits' "Mrs. Brown You've Got a Lovely Daughter," when it felt so good to know at least someone did. The reason for not being a classicist as a teen didn't matter. Anything that gave him the upper hand was justification to take it.

Ironically, Joan Baez's father was at the monastery that day. I thought my father would walk away from someone with the audacity to have brought a folk artist into the world instead of a classical quartet, but they had worked together in Paris. The man had apparently come to recuperate from what was, to him, his daughter's deeply disturbing public protest against the war in Vietnam. I think he was concerned for her welfare in a very tumultuous time, but a daughter who did not live up to expectation for whatever reason was something with which my father could identify; after all, I was standing right next to him. The implication hit home, as intended, but what really caught my attention was their mutual concern over the moral decay in America, exemplified not by a war which was killing tens of thousands for no reason—but by *Joan and me*.

It wasn't true, but what could a young girl do, caught in a monastery, not to mention a time warp? There was no point in saying countless other Americans weren't following conventional thought; my father never allowed any protest against his views. Besides, he was inexorably pleased to be an expatriot any day, but just ebullient about it when his concern over moral decay was confirmed by a man he admired. It meant, to him, that he was right to have left America: he had successfully outwitted the contamination of ethical collapse as if it were a plague he might otherwise catch.

"What is wrong with this picture?" Oh, yes. Abandon a wife, a child, *and* a country. That's morally upright.

All in all, his 18th-century moral stance in France was a mind-boggling counterpoint to the 1960's I had left behind in the United States. It was, too, such an intellectual deviation from the selfless and effortless knowledge of the Golden Girl I knew deep within to be true that I didn't take him seriously. I just wondered in passing how he thought he was going to get me into a corset of moral constriction from his adopted period when bra-burning freedom was about to become the rage in mine.

Well, this is how he did it:

Under the guise of alleged honesty, he agreed to my staying three months, but lied about my being in his legal custody, confiscated my passport on an insidious ruse and kept me captive for three years. He made sure I never had an allowance, harbored "for safe keeping" any money sent to me from California and appointed himself sole arbiter of how it could be spent. He judged my intuitive thinking as an untenable failure of the 18th-century ideal and, in deference to "rational" thought, pledged to mold me in its image.

My mother may have been out of control, but my father was perversely in control.

Although never stated, he wouldn't let me attend the American School in Paris because it was too risky; I might make English-speaking friends and, in a real *tour de force*, run away. It was a constant thought, but where could I go without money or a passport? Hitch-hiking would only take me as far as the English Channel, and how far can anyone really swim? Still, the possibility of my escaping was a persistent concern, but only because it would reflect so badly on him. I was already forbidden to seal a letter home before he read it and then virtually rewrote it by saying, "You don't want to upset your mother. Just tell her happy things." I did, not understanding that he was in a one-sided ego-competition with her, too, and did not want me contradicting his weekly written reports to her about how well he, unlike she, was parenting.

And he was parenting about as well as Mussolini. He ordered me to the attic every day to study French in isolation after an incredibly tedious time listening to it all day. The solitary confinement was punctuated by the painful impotence of not being home to help my little brother or my mother, but there I stayed until he returned from work in Paris at nine every night, under penalty of being sent to a French boarding school where "You'll wash your face in ice water and have no one to cook a hot breakfast, if you don't." I did.

I also searched his books to see where he got that one, never found it, and grimly walked four miles round trip to the local girls' lycee every day. My father insisted that going there would test my "mettle and grit," and, considering the distance, my marathon walking. Well, *quelle surprise, Papa*. While he wanted me to behave like Mamie Eisenhower, all that walking made me look like Mamie Van Doren. It confused even me, because there I was, an attractive, seemingly self-assured adolescent compelled to act like a former first lady in a series of gritty tests set up by an 18th-century attitudinarian in a language I didn't know.

"What is wrong with this picture?"

Oh, yes. Everything.

All I learned the entire school year is 1) if you look like Mamie Van Doren but act like Mamie Eisenhower, no one will like you, and 2) if you stare out of a classsroom at a bare tree long enough, it sprouts leaves; if you stare even longer, they all fall off. I could *not* understand anything else and, until Divine Mother brought it up decades later, I certainly didn't understand that I was there to test, too. As it turned out and as positive karma decreed, my job in Paris, the city of light, was to offer God to my father.

I felt very abandoned by *any* higher power in France, but still had faith that God existed. I devoured the religious stories in "Guideposts" sent by my grandfather and a friend from Young Life, a Christian organization for teens I had joined in California. And because my father refused to take us to the American Cathedral in Paris for services even on Christmas Day, I took my little sister to a French Catholic church down the street every Sunday when you know I didn't understand a thing the priest said.

I tried to show my father the way and really could not do otherwise; God was the only stability in an environment so defective and ill-intentioned that I literally shook with the fear it would send me over the edge. Still, despite the sincere efforts, my father had found agnosticism applauded in this period of social upheaval somewhere in *The New Yorker* (his token commitment to current time), refused the gift of God out of hand, curtailed the trips to the church down the street, and went right on testing.

It is no wonder my generation protested against the establishment, but there wasn't time to think about that, which probably gave a point to the testing. If my mind were on the correct conjugation of French verbs, it would not enter my head to gather up the peasants for the real meaning of 18th-century France to me: a revolution. It was pointless otherwise. After my mother, I had the mettle of mush, the grit of watered-down gruel, and that weakened state made me a sitting duck for the next round of explosives about to fly my way, ones I not only had to hear regularly but was expected to believe:

᠅ "Fathers don't have the luxury of being a friend."

I fought hard against that one, even though it was self-evident in this household. I wanted him to listen to how I felt about things, but—

᠅ "Only thinking is important. Anyone can *feel*."

The last word was always stated with the same slime in his voice as that left by the last living creature ever to have had a feeling, some ancient, amphibious ancestor crawling out of the churning waters of liquid emotion to the safety of rational thought, however rudimentary, on dry land. The real reason emotional expression was denied, of course, is that he couldn't handle it, particularly when it came from Mademoiselle Van Doren sitting so demurely in his parlor. How could a man of his rigidity possibly deal with *her*?

It must have been hard, actually, when his emotional imagery was so limited. He and my stepmother had used the endearment "love bug," but over the years left out the most critical word and actually referred to one another as "Bug"... just "Bug." This gave constant rise at the dinner table to the vision of two giant grasshoppers convivially passing the potatoes while simultaneously extending their long feelers for any opposition, like a sane thought, to the strict governing of this insect colony they kept madly calling a family.

✎ "Since you never had a real family, you must emulate ours."

Even though I got the drift of his unthinkable intent, I had to look up the word emulate. The use of an extensive vocabulary was not only mandatory in exhibiting the keen intelligence he intimated I had somehow not inherited, but a critical element in his manipulation. If I didn't know what he meant, maybe I'd be fool enough to do it.

✎ "Children are like an empty blackboard."

Having assumed a personality from literary fiction, my father believed it was possible to write the character of his choice all over my free will and I would simply act it out as an adult. Since I had been severely scribbled on by my mother toward whom I still felt an inordinate allegiance, hope for me was slight, but, "in all good conscience," he had to try. His agenda, therefore, included doing what he said my mother had not:

✎ "Make something of you."

That's when I panicked. I wasn't an inanimate blackboard and I was *not* about to be remolded into an 18th-century bug. The Golden Girl, who had peeked out for this one, bolted, when anybody could tell by the way he wielded his chalk and eraser he hadn't a clue what he was doing—but there wasn't anybody. My stepmother was useless. She actually beat up their nine-year-old son one afternoon when he refused to practice the violin.

I panicked, too, because wanting to make something of me was absolutely untrue. If my father offered opportunities to succeed, but I *failed*, then leaving me before my birth would be as justified in his mind as abandoning America—just as my mother's condition now proved the wisdom of having left her.

And my father was a maestro at orchestrating failure. Very homesick, I wanted to call home on Christmas Eve, but my father, with the unforgettably sick smile of a set-up, said, "If they want to talk to you, they'll call." What he did not say is that my mother and stepfather were divorcing and selling the house. That was the real reason I *could not* return, or be returned, to California. But he let me believe no one there cared for me because I waited by the phone well into Christmas Day and of course they never called.

He later gave me a writing assignment on the French novel of my choice. With waning hope of rescue from California, I began seeking approval from the abuser. The essay was done perfectly and in French as a surprise to please him. When that could not be criticized, my father turned around and blasted me for what he deemed to be the morally inferior selection of the novel, *Bonjour Tristesse*.

In retrospect, it was a pretty apt title; I hadn't been happy in France for a second. He did not see the humor in that, however, because he had none, but then I did not see the humor in what happened next because there was none. I was feeling very ill one morning and naturally went back to bed. When my stepmother informed my father I wasn't on the way to school, he ran up the stairs, burst into my room, literally ripped the covers off me and the bed, and said,

 "*I'll* decide when you're sick—"

—just as he would decide everything, like whether I was trying to do well in an impossible school situation. For instance, we had a young German au pere who had moved in just prior to my arrival and she was not fulfilling her position as well as my father expected. Aware that she and I had formed a friendship on the basis of our both being in an unfamiliar country and family at the same time, he informed my stepmother one morning at breakfast:

 "We have to let her go, Bug," before turning to me and adding with his sick smile, "That's what happens to people who don't try."

The blood in my veins iced. By that point I knew the house in California had been sold and the divorce would soon be final. *I had nowhere to go.* I was totally dependent on the will of a man commanding me not only to endorse but become a reality which fit nothing but an ill-informed intellectual bias and one in which personal expression contrary to accepted doctrine was judged insubordination—and it made me reel. But even worse, because of these conditions and the vulnerable state in which I had arrived after living with my mother, the part of me that first separated with the sexual abuse had by now come to believe my father: I was inadequate, undeserving, a loser—but what I was really losing again, only this time with a different parent, was myself.

Still, when my father decided my summer vacation would be spent in Paris attending a school of language immersion, the Alliance Française, a way appeared to begin the reclamation. Without a word to anyone, I skipped school every day and used my lunch money to take the Metro to Notre Dame, the Jeu de Paume and the Louvre.

I prayed for release in the cool quiet of the cathedral, fused with the color in the stained glass windows, and gathered peace in the lighting of candles. I was revitalized by the vibrant colors of Bonnard at the Jeu de Paume, and fell in love with the exquisite light of Monet and Renoir. At the Louvre, there was healing in the grandeur of the archetypes in art; divinity in sculpture; loving grace in paintings like Da Vinci's of Saint Anne as she tenderly rests her arm around her beloved daughter Mary; cherubim angels depicted repeatedly over the centuries; a hundred Christs adorned with golden haloes, and skies of blue and pinkish hue opening up into the glorious light of God.

Reconnecting with God, no matter what, became the goal—and that goal became my salvation. In the end, isn't that what it really means to make something of yourself?

Waterloo

The prayers were answered. My father was offered a job on Wall Street, which he accepted for a year, and I was allowed to go to Ashford School for Girls, a boarding school located in Ashford, Kent, England, to take A (Advanced) Level courses. The two years there passed in relief for me because my mother was released from Norwalk State Mental

Hospital; and then in absolute rapture when it turned out to be so much easier being sequestered with my peers taking A-levels than imprisoned by my father taking the heat.

I loved the Renaissance and the Reformation, Henry VIII and Elizabeth I, Milton and Shakespeare, and visits to Canterbury Cathedral to follow the tales of Chaucer and the history of Henry II and Becket; becoming a prefect in charge of the younger girls; Anglican services in our smart Sunday suits; visiting an old lady in the parish each week; wearing navy school uniforms and hats on the high street, and complaining like everyone else about kippers for breakfast and gooseberries for sweet. There were meaningful friendships, escapades substituting soap powder for sugar on corn flakes or playing field hockey in the mud before ever mastering the rules, and, above all, the freedom to begin *being* myself.

What I didn't know then was an importance in the location of the school that could not have been foreseen. In some unexpected twists to this story you will read about later, Divine Mother would lead me to karmic information about Ashford, Canterbury, Kent and England far more remarkable than "happening" to attend school there.

In the meantime, it was learned my second year that an SAT Achievement test in a science was required for university in the United States. Having found applied physics a tad difficult at the French lycee when I couldn't even apply the language, a science had to be learned from scratch. To that end, I accumulated a knowledge of biology by myself, over a four week vacation in France after my father's return, that would not only enable me to mate pigs at will should the need arise, but score an amazing 664 out of 800 on the test. While that did earn my father's approval, it did nothing to change his attitude, making what happened next his *coup d'etat* and my very unexpected Waterloo.

Final exams were held in England at the end of the two years. Pursuant to my father, no concessions were made for me; the independent board in London grading the written A-level exams would not be informed I was American.

The school was concerned that the board would not understand my different vocabulary, spelling and syntax, but my father was not—nor did I realize what he was setting up. Having scored well on prior school tests, it just seemed like a "grit and mettle" matter, not a mandate for disaster.

As it turned out, he had added poison to a situation that might have proven fatal anyway, because no one knew until after the exams that I had contracted Glandular Fever during them. Despite the memory loss, confusion, extreme fatigue, sore throat, swollen glands and body aches that are so symptomatic of the illness, I carried on through the last exam—and then collapsed. Weeks in the school infirmary passed in a haze of delirium. The nurse was a wonderful, loving woman and I cried when it was time to leave her, time to end such otherwise happy years in England by returning to France for a last summer with my father.

He usually preferred to meet me at the train station in Paris with my stepmother as a buffer between us, but this time he was ominously alone. He did not speak as we carried the bags to the car. I finally had to ask what was wrong and in that one miserable moment he said in dismissive disgust that I had failed an exam. My shock was interpreted as an act, his mind set on this single result *proving* I had never tried at all. He then refused to do what I did not know how to do from France: find out if, despite my being American, despite the illness (never an excuse to him), there had been a file error, a grade error or even a human error other than mine. Instead of trying to help, my father decided no one in the family could talk to me—and no one did.

Being with all of them at meals while they talked to one another, but ignored me, was meant to underscore what I had given up by "wasting every opportunity we have given you." It was as hurtful as he intended, and intensified by my stepmother coldly swishing her skirt out of the way without a word if we passed each other carrying plates from the dining room into the kitchen and might otherwise touch. That old plague thing was back again—and was I ever it.

Nowhere was that more apparent than in the living arrangements. They had moved from the house with the attic to a large apartment. I was literally ostracized by being banished to separate quarters with a separate entrance next door—the maid's room. The symbolism was not lost on me. I wasn't allowed to leave, nor could I. It was a security building to which I was given no key; once out was locked out. The enforced isolation over the entire summer meant there was no contact with the outside world, not even a radio.

I could cope with the restrictions, finding much more difficult the fact that while there was a sink in my room, there was no toilet. This meant having to stand every morning with my ear pressed to their front door trying to hear if someone was up. I would then have to knock and ask to be let in to use the one bathroom. Only a paper-thin wall separated the toilet from my father's head-board in the adjoining bedroom where he invariably stayed late in bed, awake.

In addition to all that had happened with him in the past, it was extremely embarrassing to know he heard these private matters, and emblematic of the real humiliation going on all along: he was privy to everything about me under penalty of a French boarding school and then degraded it until I was degraded. He was as psychologically invasive and violating as my mother had been sexually, and he, too, had done this to a daughter who truly loved him.

Like the note she left in the car ignoring my very existence, and like so many of the quotations included in this chapter, my father crystallized his contempt for me in his own hand when he penned this line: "You'll end up in the May Company basement—where you probably belong."

Ironically, it was the end of the "Summer of Love" in America, and that is when I was finally allowed to return to my country, such a disgrace to the human race it had been certified in writing.

4

Beginning to Re-Awaken

L ike most of us, I did not realize Divine Mother's hand had never left mine any more than St. Anne's arm had left its protective repose around the shoulder of her beloved daughter Mary in Da Vinci's painting at the Louvre. But I did know *something* was afoot when She silently began making positive changes in my life. Hardship would come in the future, as you will see, but it could not have been tolerated without Her intercession at this point, one marking my first steps on the return road to Her and the joy we each experienced as light long ago.

My father had frequently verbalized his plans for my siblings to attend the best private colleges on the East Coast but envisioned me mopping up the basement of the May Company in a contemporary rendition of Cinderella: the unwanted servant girl recently released from the maid's room, condemned to cleaning while her stepsisters dressed for the Ivy League ball.

To prove it, I was only allowed to apply to the University of California, and he made it clear the correct campus choice was Davis in Northern California since it would keep me far from my mother in Los Angeles. As for a UC campus at all, he said, "the money saved on you will help pay for the other children at Harvard and Yale." It was one of his more choking statements, and as difficult as the inequity was to swallow—he made it sound as if I would be chewing on a chicken bone in the cellar while others feasted on a banquet in the great hall—I was hungry for knowledge and didn't mind cleaning homes to help pay for it.

After adjusting to life in 1967 America, like the sexual revolution which had exploded in my absence, I met UC Davis Vice Chancellor Little and his wife Marian. Their surname is misleading because their compassion and generosity are huge. For no reason other than love and the grace of Divine Mother, they took me in as their own and I regard their faith in me as sacred. Marian, whose name is a conjunction of Mary and Anne in Da Vinci's painting, proved an incomparable mother; and, when my name kept appearing on the Dean's List, the Vice Chancellor, ever the good father, supported my seeking higher academic ground.

Vassar College had always been my private dream, but deeply discouraged by my father's attitude toward what he considered his witless daughter, I lost courage at the last minute and threw the application away the day it came. Yet sitting at the desk that evening, the light in the room noticeably changed. I did not know then that Divine Mother can, and often does, signal Her presence in this manner. I just knew that the shift in light caused my gaze to turn toward the wastebasket and reconsider. *Vassar was my heart's desire.* Retrieving the application, I filled it out and mailed it in.

Vassar responded by telegram, saying: "You want to be a writer. Send samples." I did. Soon another telegram came by phone. Before the Western Union operator could speak, I asked, "Good news or bad?" She laughed, "Looks good to me—'Happy to offer you a place in Vassar's class of 1971,'" and *quelle surprise, Papa*, a scholarship, too.

I went on the wings of victory, and what a gift Vassar proved to be. It was a true alma mater, because the years spent there mothered my soul by confirming an intelligence otherwise ruthlessly disparaged by my father. The rest of his influence, and my mother's, would not be so readily neutralized, but there is inescapable value now to their difficult legacy—if my negative karma with them had been slight, what point could Divine Mother make by erasing it? But if it were extreme, and then erased, what point could She *not* make?

As She had totally turned my head around about my intelligence, Her magnificence would continue in a spiritually spectacular way when my grandfather died during my junior year at Vassar. On hearing the news, I flew from New York to California, and this is the truly extraordinary story of what transpired with him in April, 1970.

Life After Death

Sitting alone the evening before the funeral, the wind suddenly rustled the bushes outside, causing the leaves to scratch against the windowpane. That caught my attention, but it was nothing compared to my grandfather who, in the next moment, and in spirit, silently placed himself around my shoulders like a comforting cloak, supporting me from behind and telepathically asking for forgiveness.

I was stunned by his unexpected arrival, but so very pleased he had come. As he had once wracked his brain, pacing about the little house in San Gabriel trying to figure out the identity of Madre, I now wracked my brain trying to figure out why he would possibly need forgiveness.

Looking back, certainly he was sorry for not having prevented the abuse from my mother, but I am positive today that he was seeking forgiveness for having so jauntily side-stepped Divine Mother in his own living room when I was little, counting buttons. Just because She was invisible to him then didn't mean She wasn't vivid to him now.

Sensing he could not otherwise find freedom, I offered forgiveness for whatever he thought he might have done. Grandpa then indicated there would be someone attending the funeral for me to speak with and in some way help; would I? Anything for you, Grandpa. He next relayed the news, and it was news to me, that I would have a wonderful life—and with that, he left.

The identity of the person became instantly apparent at the funeral: my grandfather's brother and virtual carbon-copy, a man whom I had not seen since childhood. I approached him with a red rose at the cemetery and, handing it to him, explained how Grandpa had come and asked me to talk to him. With that information, he broke down and wept, because he knew what I did not yet know. Gathering himself together, he said, "Your grandfather wants you to talk with me because he came to me in a dream the night before he died and said, 'Please take care of Wendy.'"

By these two communications, the one confirming the other, Grandpa established the fact that life continues after death; telepathy is real; love and forgiveness are the answer, and taking care of each other is the way to do both. He more than returned my meager attempt to support him with faith when I was 15; he re-opened the door to heaven. And I know now that Divine Mother helped him do it.

It was with elation that adult friends were told about this pure and genuine experience, including a psychology professor at UC Davis for whom I had worked as a typist the two previous summers, and his wife, Rochelle, a psychiatric nurse I respected and had come to love during the course of babysitting their two young daughters. Certainly she would appreciate the story, but instead Rochelle said, "It's true for you, but not really true."

"What?"

"It was your experience, but it didn't really happen."

Isn't that what Galileo heard the first time he ran around telling everyone the earth revolves around the sun?

Truth can't be qualified, but I didn't know that then. I tried to give her lack of spiritual insight the merit it didn't really deserve by questioning my own perceptions, a habit which had become nearly second nature after living so long with those odd people who said they were my parents. In the end, there was advantage to such extended mental gymnastics. My thinking has personally been put to more questioning than all the contestants in the history of "Jeopardy" and no one can tell me now I don't know what I know. Yet for years I took these truths as they came along to Rochelle, to teachers, to my father, or to anyone else "in authority" for external validation. Now, that *was* pretty witless. These precious discoveries should never be subjected to confirmation by a world that still has trouble verifying all the ingredients in a hot dog.

Unable to accept Rochelle's answer, I was advised to speak with a second professor at the University, one who is now very well-known for his professional work in paranormal psychology. His cryptic response to my detailed story was so typical of reactions to come, it can't be forgotten: "I'm not interested in your story, but you have nice legs."

Granted, I think he was collecting a specific type of paranormal story for a paper he was writing, so even though my legs fit his fantasies, my experience didn't fit his format, and I was shown the door. Finding out that intelligence and a Ph.D. don't equal loving wisdom any more than intelligence and a law degree equal justice, however, did not make for a happy day. I questioned all the way home, and well into the next many years, "Where *is* justice? Where *is* loving wisdom? Where *is* real intelligence?" Unbeknownst to me, Divine Mother would one day make certain I found out.

Life in the Real World

The answers initially began when karma conspired in my falling in love with an adorable, witty, but completely wacky New York-based Parisian, Michel. When we were introduced, he had been steadily employed for ten years, married for ten years and the exemplary father of two children for ten years. There was no indication in his history that he would leave his wife six weeks after meeting me—the very surprised but only external catalyst needed to cause an already imploding relationship to collapse. What surprised me even more, of course, is that he left because he really loved me.

From my point of view, Michel was a gift from God, providing three elements which had been so lacking in my life: boundless love, unending attention, and comic relief. He was so entertaining and endearing that we were awash with good times and good humor, followed very quickly by something of equal value. Just two months after meeting him, and copied here verbatim, I wrote from the heart this highly accurate description of Divine Mother without having a clue at the time what I was doing:

What great strength in me reaches out to embrace the sun and become one with it? What great strength in me reaches out to enfold the moon and warm it into the sun? And what great strength in me knows more of the world than I know myself? What is in me to teach me? Is it me or someone else in me? Who works in me, plays in me, laughs in me, cries in me, and sees in me those things on which I verge in transcending discovery?

It's all there. All the truth. All the love. All the purity. All the strength. All the knowledge. It is in me already. It is only a matter of teaching myself and learning what it is. For now, it is something I can define in no other way except that it is in me already, only asking to be seen, to be noticed, and to be taken for what it is

I would not have time to realize Divine Mother was that presence because, mid-stream down the river of love baptizing me with such a heightened awareness of Reality, there were a few new things to learn about my Frenchman. He began, for instance, to display what would prove to be a consistent and disheartening aversion to dallying over such fundamentals as—life.

In a decade that did not yet embrace stay-at-home husbands, fathers or lovers, he enjoyed being home so much as to avoid entirely the responsibility which had been the hallmark of his character. He found ingenious ways not to work three years out of six despite the birth of our children, and developed a remarkable capacity to remain unruffled by mounting bills—but, why not? Since society was trumpeting the cause of women establishing their own credit and I had answered the call, all the bills were in my name. That aside, I think now Michel was, overall, very uncertain about the next step in a life which had taken some pretty sharp turns. Yet his not knowing where to put one foot after the other meant our moving across the country *three* different times in as many directions, being thrust into constant chaos no matter where we lived, valiantly trying to get out of whatever he got us into—and then squabbling about it.

The French love to squabble. It is a true, however bizarre, cultural form of affection. In other words, if you love someone enough to make love with them day and night, you will autmatically fill every other waking and sleeping hour bickering with them. Since Michel began following other French cultural stereotyping at this time, such as abhorring Americans (of which I was one), disrespecting women (of which I was one) and being critical of everything else in the world (of which I had to be one sometimes), my nerves unraveled fast. They started spinning around half-crazed like bees suddenly smoked out of the secure haven of their hive.

Surely Michel had come with a sign, "I am your next karmic event," but I didn't see it. Even if I had, my sense of responsibility, which canceled out his lack of one, wouldn't let me walk away, not when he had left a *family* for me. It was the strongest show of love by anyone in my life; it just came with such a hefty price tag: him.

If ever there were a case for an extra-marital affair instead of marriage or living together, we were it. But the die was cast. I buzzed about, this way and that, before making a bee-line into the safest sanctuary in sight: way, way, *way* inside myself. I was so far removed from the madness, Michel had to call me on a megaphone.

But you know what? It was pleasant in there. It was peaceful in there—*and soon I would find Divine Mother in there.* In the end Michel was not so much a detour from my spiritual quest as an impetus head-first into it just to get away from him, certainly underscoring the old adage that *everyone* in our life has a purpose.

Just so you have a fair idea of what was going on, let's

take a look at two critical blunders Michel and I made right off the bat.

The first, which I couldn't have made up in my wildest dreams, occurred a few months after we met. We moved to Dublin, Ireland where I was to attend graduate school at Trinity College—but it was too cold for even the most hardy Dubliner that year, and Michel was miserable, so it seemed a good idea to travel on to the warmer clime of France and visit Michel's childhood home in the country. After all, Michel had given up a family for me; what was giving up graduate school and my entire *future*?

We began by driving leisurely in a rented car through scenic Switzerland, meandering our way to the first French border station we chanced upon. The guard glanced at our passports, did a double-take on Michel's and sternly asked us to pull over to the side of the road. That is when Michel grabbed my arm and hissed in my ear, "They're going to put me in jail for a year. Do we stay or make a run for it?"

I didn't know what he meant, but since I hardly knew him, that wasn't alarming. The alarm came from the fact that he was vibrating behind the steering wheel in terror and had actually gone bug-eyed in a matter of seconds.

"What are you talking about?"

With his accent, the words jumbled out worse than Ricky Ricardo. "I never registered for the draft. I was in the army, sure, in America, but here, you're French until you die, but I'm a citizen of the United States and where is that paper? You know, this is bad. The police came to my father's house in Paris last year, looking for me and—

"You've known about this for a *year?*"

"Sure I've known about it. I just didn't do anything about it." His teeth chattered. "So do we run for it?"

I had been a Girl Scout. Scouts saluted and stood up to the worst. Actually, if I could have unbuckled my seat belt fast enough, I would have stood up and hit him over the head with it, but it was too late. The guard approached the car and told us to follow him to the local police station to await orders from headquarters in Paris. Since the police had no phone and were forced to rely on a rickety telex for information from the outside world, the wait was long. Bored to death, one officer actually brought in a plump brie, a few baguettes and three bottles of red wine so we all, the police included, might pass the time in the best French manner.

When the telex finally relayed its message—in code, can you believe—the news was worse than anyone expected. We had to go to Lyons, by train, to the French army induction center to meet with a general, and so we did, flanked by two police officers who played cards all the way there.

The general was a kind man who told us that French-born American citizens who had served in Viet Nam but failed to register for the draft in France—"insoumis" as all such unfortunates are called—had been inducted into the army for months before they could untangle the red tape required to release them. He suggested Michel get his physical just down the hall; I should find a hotel room and pray.

I did, and not knowing what else to do, I took a bath. That is when there was a knock at the door and Michel burst into the hotel room with a three-day pass in his hands. "I passed the physical! The general gave me this pass to take care of the rental car and get my affairs in order. Well, you're my affair and I'm ordering you to leave here with me in the rental car."

This made perfect sense to him, as most things luna-tic did, and after a few cautionary phone calls to lawyers, rich uncles and anyone else he could ask, Michel learned his first instinct had been right; except for the French Foreign Legion, there was no way out of this but to leave the country immediately. And so it was, a mere few months after graduating from Vassar, that I, who had done nothing wrong, found myself on the lam in a rental car trying to get the hell out of France and escape into Switzerland with a draft-dodger who had already served in the American army.

This may not have been a very auspicious beginning for any relationship, but it was absolutely prophetic for ours.

Even though a new French President later pardoned Michel, most of our time together was so mixed up, we might as well have been living in a blender.

As for the second critical blunder (like the first one wasn't enough), there were too many divorces in our respective families, especially with Michel's on the horizon. Since it was obvious, to us at least, that man cannot join in holy matrimony what God never separated in the first place—each of us from one another—we decided not to be redundant about it and deliberately did not marry. Of course, we could not *get* married at that point, but women's magazines in 1972 were blithely proclaiming a lack of ceremony the wave of the future. Finding this extremely convenient under the circumstances, Michel and I blithely followed along—only to find ourselves hanging out to dry. We were, forever and ever, amen, the only weddingless couple in a sea of humanity constantly at the altar.

We had been hoodwinked by *"Cosmo."*

Rather than do something about it, or live with the courage of our conviction, we created an alternative which did not exist: we *pretended* we were married. This deceit, of course, along with a few thousand others, pretty much robbed any hope of an honest way of life, but the psychological freedom inherent in secretly making no vows other than those of the heart really did do the trick—it kept us together longer than anyone, especially we, would have liked.

Intractably stubborn, with wills of ego-bound iron, neither of us would admit we had made a mistake. And we did actually, somewhere in there, really love each other. But it quickly came to pass that the once liberating pleasure of being together out of choice was experienced by suffering to death, with me shuddering into the haven of my great inner sanctuary and Michel screaming through the megaphone to come out and squabble.

Fortunately, Divine Mother had an antidote to this folly when we were obviously too dysfunctional to come up with one on our own, and that antidote was dreams.

5

Dreams:
The First Look Within

Knowledge is a birthright we cannot relinquish any more than an evergreen its color. Our reception of the continuous and natural flow of knowledge became obstructed, however, when we began to believe in the ego.

To compensate for our mistake, the Divine Meditation you will be reading about was inaugurated to convey knowledge telepathically. Still, the ego managed to convince us to turn a deaf ear even there. To recapture our attention, images were introduced into Divine Meditation, each symbol a powerful nugget of truth and light communicating knowledge visually. But when we made the decision to turn a blind eye to go with our deaf ear, something we could not avoid or deny had to be instituted.

Enter dreams.

Our free will still determined if we would consciously remember them, but *having* dreams—the telepathic, visual reception of knowledge—was not an option.

Divine Mother works telepathically with our higher intelligence in dreams and Divine Meditation. She creates the images and, by the very nature of Her Being, provides the light and truth within them. The word *nightmare*, for instance, derives from *mere*, which in French means mother. A nightmare is impacting because of the power in the images and telepathy Divine Mother sends to alert us to very important information we have otherwise resisted knowing.

This means no critical life event is ever as sudden as it seems. I recently found a 1982 nightmare that I had written in my dream journal but never interpreted because the images were so frightening, as they should have been—step by step they detailed a near-death you will be reading about, one which occurred *seven* years later in 1989.

For our own protection and a one-up advantage, we are *always* alerted well in advance and many times after to a situation, event or condition by a variety of different dream stories—*all with the same underlying theme*. If the sheer repetition does not open our eyes to something in need of attention, a nightmare ensues in order to wake us up to it.

Whether dreams are magnified into a nightmare or not, they are invariably giving us the opportunity to:

(1) assimilate the information, prepare for it, or take time to adjust to it;

(2) pinpoint the problem;

(3) or, if we cannot pinpoint the problem on our own, talk with Divine Mother about what must be changed in our lives and/or in ourselves to alter the current path in favor of a different outcome. Had I known so at the time, it is very likely the near-death could have been averted. As it was, I did have the advantage of a rigorous dress-rehearsal, which leads us to the next alternative:

(4) let the whole matter slide by ignoring the dreams or nightmares, and walk head-on into the experience.

If we do not wisely resolve the issue beforehand, but opt to let it slide, we are not necessarily destined for doom because the least dreams or nightmares do *is* provide a dress-rehearsal. Rehearse does not only mean to "repeat," but to "re*hear*(se)" or hear again; the dream is a story we definitely will hear again—on the physical plane when it actualizes in daily life. When it does, we will have the great benefit of being familiar with it and we will most likely create a resolution like the one given in the dream or nightmare whether we consciously remember it or not.

Of course dreams serve a variety of other functions. Divine Mother makes sure they are also harmonious, calming, humorous and uplifting, as well as an encyclopedia of information of every kind and dimension, from the activities of daily life to our spiritual, emotional, physical, and mental status and purpose—past, present and future—on this plane or on another. As the one form of incoming intelligence we can't control, they are substantial and vital contributors to our Divine evolution.

Above all, however, dreams are so permeable as to allow constant access to Divine Mother, and She to us, which means we have *always* had contact with Her. This contact is the bridge of grace closing the gap in awareness between the unconscious and conscious minds; between direct knowledge and knowing in part; between Reality and our perception of it, and between Divine Mother and Her children.

Before the advent of the ego, no gap existed; the unconscious and conscious minds were one and the same. But the ego made a makeshift place for itself, that gap as it were, creating the illusion of two minds. This automatically interfered with our reception of the natural flow of Divine communication, and distorted our perception of Reality to fit the ego's agenda of deception and denial. In this role, the ego is also known as the subconscious: the lid on what is otherwise uninterrupted knowledge, the filter that allows only tiny grains of truth into consciousness while keeping the great ones back.

The ego/subconscious mind functions as judge and jury. In the brief time it takes to awaken from sleep, for example, it can and does misinterpret, misinform or write off as fantasy what is otherwise delivered in dreams for our own good: knowledge, truth, light and intelligence; warnings, approval, blessings and karmic information from past lives, as well as guidance, motivation, and communication with beings from this side or the other—all in the form of symbols, images, themes, scenes, stories, characters and dialogue.

Particularly significant dreams began after my grandfather's death. Their regularity increased to such an extent when we started trying to have a baby that I began the previously mentioned dream journal in the summer of 1972, as well as a journal for the baby we very much wanted to have. The dreams became intensely vivid with the pregnancy and were so evocative after Tyler's birth in 1973 that my attention was fully engaged with the unconscious and the indisputable fact that every image in a dream, just like Divine Mother, is a teacher of truth.

Once I developed an understanding of the symbolism, the dreams proved consistently accurate and just as humorous. In one, Michel was the Captain and I the second mate, castaway on a sinking ship. That was a pretty graphic interpretation of exactly what was going on, particularly the pun; following his first marriage, I literally was Michel's second mate. Further, our relationship had occurred, in part, because I was unconsciously trying to work out through him much of what had been imposed by my identically French-minded father. This meant, however, that instead of swimming away to freedom as planned, I had actually boarded the Titanic by choosing an equally stifling man. To prove it, Monsieur le Capitain tried to suffocate me in the dream by stuffing me into a ditty bag.

The dreams presented very vivid views of the alternative: trees like giant bouquets blossoming in pink, blue or lavendar flowers, tropical fruits growing in sweet-scented abundance and Christ-like men communing tenderly with me. I would awaken in the morning with deepest yearning as my response to this Divine call back to Eden, yet find myself in a relationship of sickening contrast.

It was a daily ritual to dodge Michel's insights into negative attributes, so piercingly accurate they could knock you off your feet like a dart gun, because he didn't have the courtesy to temper them with—what's that word he always forgot? Oh, yes, *compassion.* His paranormal ability was to be commended, but my dreams, which he could not control, were perceived as unwanted competition. Once, as I was relating a clairvoyant dream to a friend at home, he casually strolled behind my chair and bent down to look for something—or so we thought. Instead, he suddenly stood up and yanked off my 1970's hair piece as if I were Samson and he could actually de-wig me of my spiritual strength.

Michel's family of origin was not superior to mine, so we were truly adrift when it came to behavior better than his insults or my submission to them. We had been raised in the fine art of denigration and were compulsively acting it out. This was a down-spiraling situation until a series of graded dream lessons from Divine Mother came to the rescue.

At first the grades were a discouraging yet accurate D or F, but as I learned from the dreams and my self-esteem increased, they rose to B's and A's. Once they did, I had the courage to start standing up for myself, stop wearing hairpieces Michel could rip off, and refuse to tolerate such treatment or the dishonesty we shared.

Dreams with a Twist

Truth continued in the dreams, but in ways that were to reveal a hint of the larger reality we all share when we are willing to see it, a hint that would soon be confirmed in real time.

In a startling series of dreams earlier, in 1969 at UC Davis, a newspaper had been presented. Instead of the conventional black type on white paper, however, the type was white-gold, shimmering vividly against a black background. This was so unusual that I thought it must be a marker in the dream series asking me to pay attention to what would follow.

It was a marker, but it was also the way we may, and I do now, literally "read" Divine Mother in Divine Meditation. Besides coming in telepathically, the words are written out one by one in the white-gold type of Her light on the dark background of the skein of time and space. She was just re-entering consciousness at Davis through a visual format that would not be actualized without the dreams for a number of years to come.

Since a newspaper in a dream means prophecy, this one dream had three very different, but equally valid, meanings. Dreams are invariably this inclusive and economical, as is the universe itself. If more than one purpose can be thrown in for the price of one, it will be. Nothing is as either/or as our minds perceive it. There are always multiple interpretations and choices, each one significant in its own right.

In what turned out to be a prophetic dream immediately following the one about the newspaper, for example, I was riding down a dirt road on the back of a buckboard in an earlier century. My grandfather, dead, was in a casket in the back. To the left was a meadow, the leaves of the trees high on the hill above turning from a bright green to shocking pink and back to green again. To the right, a woman in white cap and apron was baking bread in a brick oven built next to the fireplace. What made the dream memorable was the play of color on the trees and the unusual placement of the oven, but what made it meaningful is this:

At the end of 1973 and at my insistence—although not knowing why other than feeling it was important to live there—Michel, Baby Ty and I moved to Massachusetts. I began modeling the following year, and one Saturday a photographer drove me to a shoot in Sudbury at an establishment built during the early 1700's, the Wayside Inn.

I had brought along a book about clairvoyant dreams to read on the way. It quickly became a topic of conversation—in which the photographer had absolutely no interest. He was a nice older man who grunted at the concept of clairvoyance in dreams or anywhere else. Soon, however, the scenery began to look very familiar to me, especially a broken-down buckboard in the middle of a meadow across the road from the Wayside Inn. Trees high on the hill above it were green but would change to pink in the New England autumn—and it all was viewed from precisely the same perspective as in the dream.

I told the photographer this, and that we would find an oven built next to the fireplace in the kitchen of the Inn. That certainly perked his interest, because, sure enough, the oven was there, directly next to the fireplace in the kitchen, the *only* original room spared by a later fire. We were then told by the innkeeper that the cook at the time would have dressed in a white cap and apron, and she would have baked bread in the oven, thus completing the dream.

We took pictures outside on the grounds, but both of us had changed. The photographer was a believer, and I? "Wendy," he said from his view through the camera lens, "you don't look like yourself anymore." In that photograph I am sitting on the white fence that fronts the meadow; behind me is the broken-down buckboard and the hill of trees. There is an ethereal quality to my face, and I *do* look like someone else. That Saturday I did not know who, but by the following Monday I did, and it came about this way:

Having had Ty without any immediate family to recommend, I wanted to know for his sake who had existed in the past. A Mormon relative had just written in response to my request for information and, since it would take her a little time to make copies of the numerous genealogical papers on the family in her possession, she suggested my locating a book on the Leavitt family at the Boston Public Library. It was key because my great-grandmother, Grandpa's mother, was named Louisa Leavitt.

I was very surprised to find the book at the library on Monday, extremely interested to learn that John Leavitt, my great-grandfather eleven generations earlier, had begun the family in America in 1642—but astonished to find in a footnote that through the Leavitts I am related to *David Howe* (b.1674), *the original owner of the Wayside Inn.* Further research showed I am Howe's tenth generation niece. (See Appendix A-1)

This means I had been sitting on the fence in front of the photographer at the Wayside Inn looking like one of my own *ancestors*, and that is why Grandpa had been dead in the dream; my genetic ties to the original owner of the Wayside Inn had come through the deceased members of his family. Also, as you will be seeing in increasing and convincing detail, we can be reborn into our own genetic line. In addition to looking like one of my own ancestors, then, I most likely was looking like myself as I actually appeared in the 1700's of the dream.

Fine with me, and so was this, one of the twists promised to you about my attending Ashford School for Girls in Ashford, Kent, England: John Leavitt, my great-grandfather all those generations back, not only emigrated to America from England, but an astounding number of our mutual, direct-line ancestors were *born and lived* in Ashford, Kent, England. In a very real way, then, I didn't just go to school there; I went home.

I discovered, too, that John Leavitt and many other relatives had lived and were buried in Hingham, Massachusetts, *ten minutes* from where we were living in Marshfield. Not only does Leavitt Street exist in Hingham, but the original Leavitt Homestead stands near the library, replete with a plaque bearing the family name. Divine Mother had truly brought me home in so many ways, in so many places, and I never would have known it without that one dream.

But there is more. I just recently learned that Louisa Leavitt's grandmother (my great-great-great-grandmother), Sarah Sturdevant Leavitt, had a short autobiography published in the book, *Our Pioneer Heritage*. She writes that as a young woman she was informed "by the voice of the Spirit ... so loud, clear and plain to my understanding that I knew a way would be opened for us" to go west with the founder of the Mormon Church, Joseph Smith, to Nauvoo, Illinois. A way indeed opened. When Smith was later murdered, it was revealed to Sarah in a *dream* that she and the family must leave immediately or be killed, too. They did leave, this time following Smith's successor and, although I don't believe they knew it then, *their own relative*, Brigham Young. They joined his first wagon train party west to Utah in 1847. (See Appendix A-1)

Mormonism came to a close in my immediate family with Grandpa's wavering faith. However, without Sarah becoming Mormon, and the vast genealogical records kept by the Mormon Church, I would not have access to the names, dates and places of my family's history to which my dreams were so intimately connected—nor would I know that my great-great-great-grandmother Sarah also wrote about her spiritual experiences, was aware of her clairvoyant dreams, and was deeply conscious of and receptive to Divine telepathy. The similarities she and I share, ones I did not know until now, are a strong indication that individuals are born into the genetic pool needed to accommodate their karmic goals and obligations as precisely as possible.

What this specifically means is that the soul is drawn to the genes for intelligence, physical attributes, health concerns or benefits, emotional tendencies, talents, abilities and the like that will provide the positive karmic situations and conditions one has earned, as well as the negative karma to be worked out in a particular lifetime. Since we are continuously working on our karma over many lifetimes, adding and deleting as we go, the best "suit" of genes to wear is often a variation of those we have worn before. Being reborn into the same family line is often the most efficient way to do that. Our genes are not a random selection or the luck of the draw, but a personally tailored creation chosen to conform our life circumstances to the soul's requirements.

As another example of that being true, many pilgrims preceded the pioneers in my family. Four direct-line ancestral families were on the Mayflower and lived in Plymouth Colony, a place we often visited as it too was only ten minutes away. Having felt all my life like a pilgrim in the spiritual pursuit of Divine Mother, and a pioneer in search of Her in the West, this kind of genetic heritage fits like a glove.

For someone who grew up believing she had no heritage to speak of, this was good stuff to be sure, but hardly an end to clairvoyant dreams and enlightening encounters. Divine Mother had far more up Her sleeve on that score. As you will see later, the dream about the Wayside Inn, and my connection to it, was still only the *beginning* of one of the most remarkable stories of all.

6

Telepathy

The telepathy experienced with Divine Mother in childhood, and openly returned by Grandpa after his death, continued with an insistent knocking on my head by someone on the other side very intent on being born in the next five minutes if that could please be arranged. Since I wasn't even pregnant, that feat did require some attention.

I wanted another baby, but when my period suddenly came twice in one month—as if to say that knocking soul needed to be heeded, and in a hurried manner to meet a certain date—it was agreed to sooner than later. At the time, however, I was so disillusioned with the world and virtually everyone's inability to find lasting happiness in it, that I sat down and specifically prayed for a child who, like Ty, not only had a handle on this thing called life, but would be an example to others of how to do it right.

Linc was born in 1976 and in a half hour, on December 22—the first full day of increasing light in the world. Making that symbolic deadline had been part of the fuss, but the rest he delivered himself: lying in my arms only moments after his birth, he looked straight into my eyes and reminded me of that prayer, quite forgotten by then, when he said telepathically and so clearly I can hear it all these years later, "I'm the one you've waited for."

Linc slept through the night every night, "Yes!" was his first word and a victorious "I did it!" his first complete sentence after managing a somersault. And then there was this: when he was four, Linc needed an operation. He had a vivid dream about it one morning before a surgeon had been selected or even recommended by his pediatrician. At my request, Linc drew a picture of what he had seen.

Looking at the drawing carefully, I asked, "What is that near the operating table?"

"An ashtray."

"There was an ashtray in your dream about the operation?"

"Yes."

As it turned out, the surgeon recommended to us *the next day* by the pediatrician, and the one who did the surgery, was named: *Dr. Ash.*

In addition to this open third-eye connection to light and truth, which included receiving an interior green light alarm in response to something negative or a pink light go-ahead when it was good, Linc cannot abide injustice, does not tolerate illusion and has been an extraordinary example all his life to the one person I hadn't prayed for him to come into the world to help: me.

Without specific prayer, Ty has proven an example of another kind. He has always felt at ease in his own skin; he passed through the terrible twos better than any nay-sayer on earth without losing the ability in adulthood when it was needed; he has flowed along unfazed through all the ups and downs of life with the acceptance of real wisdom, and he can manifest at will:

The Christmas he was six, Ty wanted to race in competition and asked Santa Claus for a dirt bike. Separated at that point, neither Michel nor I could afford such an expensive item. We tried to tell Ty the chances were slim Santa would bring the bike, but he *would not stop believing in its reality.* I tried to cushion the blow on Christmas Eve, but he set a place for Santa with his brother, complete with cookies and milk, added a bottle of Pepto Bismol for good measure, and went to bed in full anticpation of the bike being there the next day. As I had feared, there was no bike in the morning—*but the money for it was.* A man had appeared at Michel's door on Christmas Eve and purchased an old set of bedroom furniture for the exact amount of the bike. Ty bought it the next day. And the races? He came in first so many times it was embarrassing.

Ty and Linc clearly arrived with their access to inner knowing intact at birth—as we all do. By the time Linc came along, I was alert enough to realize that inner knowing was how they handled things so well, but I had to relearn how to access it in adulthood—as we all do. At this point I didn't have conscious contact with Divine Mother, the source of all inner knowing, but I was about to receive a clue to Her whereabouts—and it involved both children and telepathy.

A Clue to Divine Mother: The Inner Child

The first instance promising direct access to Divine Mother occurred in 1977 after a series of traumatic events following our move from Massachusetts to California. Linc was barely eight months old and Ty had just turned four.

Being with Michel, in or out of my sanctuary, had become intolerable and, thanks entirely to a small inheritance from my stepfather's mother, I finally had the money to put action behind my words of discontent. Michel retaliated at a permanent separation by saying, "Come on, Ty. Mommy doesn't want us anymore." He said he was taking Ty with him to find an apartment, but instead drove him to Vermont as hostage, laying out the terms for his release over the phone: "Let me come back, and you can have Ty back."

No words describe the grief of a mother who loses a living child. Michel's act of vengeance was unheard of then, not the frequent ploy it is today—according to the Center for Missing and Exploited Children, 350,000 children are annually abducted by a family member. To my knowledge, an equivalent agency did not exist then, and there were no role models. Not having Divine Mother consciously at hand to ask, I didn't know what to do but follow my stepfather's advice: leave Michel alone and he would bring Ty home.

The only way I could do that without going insane from the pain was to internalize the loss, but I did it too well and developed what the doctors finally termed a "mystery" illness. It wasn't recognized for many years as a return of the Glandular Fever that I had first experienced in England and would disastrously suffer again in the future.

Linc wasn't faring any better. He was quickly hospitalized with severe diarrhea, which surely came about in response to my grief as well as his own over the sudden separation from his father and brother—more than half his family had disappeared overnight and he felt, he said years later, they hadn't cared enough to take him, too. Because the pediatrician didn't know the physical cause of Linc's illness, he was put in the isolation ward. I couldn't even touch him—and now two sons were out of reach.

All of this seemed such an unbearable price to pay for wanting a life of integrity that I literally went into shock. It was as if I had suddenly been dropped down a well with cotton padding over my ears. I could not understand what people said; their words echoed. I got into my car in this condition, drove directly from the hospital to a neighboring store and stole a blazingly bright blue sweater and photographs of Ty just developed from negatives Michel had sent from Vermont for me to see what I was missing.

I was instantly arrested. The charge was reduced to trespassing and, due to the circumstances, put under seal by the judge so no one would know, but I tell the story now to illustrate what pain makes people do without access to Divine Mother, and to explain the symbolism, as relevant as if it were in a nightmare instead of just feeling like one.

In regard to the blue sweater, clothes represent the attitudes or feelings we are "wearing" or expressing at a given time; they also symbolize protection. Blue is the color of our protection, Divine Mother, as well as the color of communication, peace, and unhappiness ("I'm blue"). The intensity of color is important because it emphasized every aspect of blue at play here—I was screaming inside for God to stop the madness; I needed Divine protection; I had to communicate my feelings but no one could understand the pain; there was no peace, and I had *never* been so unhappy.

Symbolically, I stole the photographs of Ty because he had been stolen from me. Michel had sent me the negatives of the pictures, just as negatives were what he had sent me in our relationship until it had to stop. In that regard, the arrest, a word which literally means "to stop," has additional meaning in this context: I needed everything—Ty's abduction, my illness, Linc's illness, Michel's negatives, my relationship with him, and the separation from the God I was screaming for—to just *stop.*

And this is how it did:

The inner strength developed from the dreams with Divine Mother took over. I sat with myself for days to face head-on the errors of my life. Not a single one escaped scrutiny, from the sheer idiocy of committing myself to Michel after knowing him six weeks to having taken mental and emotional battering from him and his two antecedents: my mother and father. I would *not* live with abuse anymore. I could see what it had done to me, and that it would just be passed on to my children, as it had been already to Ty by being separated from his mother, and to Linc by being separated from his brother and father. I could see, too, that karma was passed down in a family as readily as genes—and it was hitting us like bricks.

Unwilling to accept Michel's compromise, I decided to wait with the integrity of being true to myself. The wait became the longest six months of my life during which I was constantly threatened that if I did anything to retrieve Ty, Michel would take him to France where it would be impossible to find or reclaim him. Knowing that Michel did not have any paternal rights to Ty in Massachusetts because we weren't married, I banked on that being true in Vermont when I ultimately made the decision to override Michel's threats and not allow him to disempower me: I would go to Vermont, find the local sheriff and get my son.

Fearing he might be alerted, no one was told of my intention, yet Michel called a few days later and offered to bring Ty back—which he did, and didn't stay himself. I know the decision not to give in and my *willingness* to take action were key in turning the lock that opened the door for Ty to come home. Across the miles and over the air waves, internal determination alone had changed Michel's mind.

There were additional benefits to not giving in. First, I had to know personally that my commitment to my own integrity was unbreakable. Strength, integrity and commitment are truly innate qualities, the jewels of the soul, but with an ego constantly in the way, most of us only become keenly conscious of them through a means my father had ironically and perfectly prepared me for: *testing*. The universe tests us in moments of crisis *to prove to us* what we are entirely capable of in ordinary circumstances: being strong, honest and committed. It is part of waking up to who we are, because when we were created in the image of God, there was nothing bargain-basement about it; like exquisite jewelry, only precious gems were used, not the fool's gold of the ego that weakness, dishonesty and disloyalty represent.

Secondly, the loss of Ty when he was a child of four, the same age I was abused by my mother, triggered an experience which helped me resist Michel and bring Ty home.

While they were gone, I enrolled in a UCLA Extension class, "At a Journal Workshop," where I and many others were taught to meditate for the first time. We were verbally led into our own inner being for whatever might transpire. I heard first a repeated, welcoming chorus of "Hello, Wendy!" This greeting was followed by something unknown to me at the time—a phenomenon only recently recognized as a universally integral part of our psychology and, I believe now, our actual being: the inner child.

The experience was very emotional because my inner child was *the Golden Girl*, myself at four, walking toward me in the sunlit garden of my childhood, a bouquet of red roses in her arms. She was so bright and happy and healthy, I cried with the relief that she had survived. When she smiled and handed me the roses, I was stunned by the symbolism of her gesture: *I loved myself.*

The Golden Girl, always connected to God, was perfect truth, love and wisdom in this form. There was much to learn through inner, telepathic dialogue with her; much strength to receive from her healing hugs; much to give in return. One day she would grow up inside of me, nurtured by someone I still had not remembered, Divine Mother.

Conscious recognition of Divine Mother would not come again until various life events culminated in a near-death, and even then Her Reality could not be *confirmed* to me until the second near-death noted in the nightmare at the beginning of the previous chapter. All of the delay and trauma involved in my re-awakening mark just how much negativity the ego had packed in over the years in its endeavor to keep me, as it endeavors to keep all of us, from the truth and light. The reunion with the Golden Girl was so threatening a step on the road back to Divine Mother that the ego would now try to take me out—literally—and since I wasn't looking, that wouldn't be too hard.

The First Near-Death

It was May, 1980 and I had just been very hurt by a former boyfriend who had briefly resurfaced from college. Wanting only to be carefree—which the ego eagerly translated into careless—I agreed to celebrate Cinqo de Mayo in Mexico with a man I scarcely knew. Not ever the slightest attraction in the 1960's, I went so far with the idea of being carefree as to eat brownies he had baked himself with marijuana, he said, but which must have contained drugs far more potent: I later learned he had been divorced for his love affair with cocaine.

Margaritas followed at the restaurant at dinner. Since drinking or trying drugs was *extremely* rare for me, their combined effect caused me to comment, "This feels so good, no wonder people do drugs." Then, out of nowhere, it all turned around; my temperature rose so high so fast that I couldn't even call out for help. I stood up from the table, weaved to the door, managed to get outside just as darkness invaded my vision and passed out cold on a side street in Ensenada.

Lying unconscious on the outside, but ultra-conscious on the inside, I zoomed into the stars and was suspended among them. Somehow the sun was shining, too, making daylight shimmer with the starlight. From this elevated perspective, an awareness that I know now was Divine Mother focused my attention on the fact that I had to return to my children. I could not leave them, not like this, and certainly not without saying goodby.

Agreeing, I suddenly found myself coming to, flat on the ground. To make sure I wasn't dead, I listened for sincerity in the voices of the people hovering over me until I, too, could believe, "She's awake! She'll be all right now."

My date from hell returned with me by taxi to the hotel where I went in and out of consciousness. Afraid of being caught with drugs and going to jail, he refused to call for help, even when he said it looked as if I were dying, and handed me a mirror to view the grim evidence myself. The dark shadow of death hung visibly over my face like a shroud and I said so. Realizing that if I did die he would not only go to jail but never leave, he finally called an ambulance. It took me to a Red Cross station the locals called a hospital and I was cared for there by being pumped with an antidote: Valium.

We had flown down to Mexico in his plane and now had to fly back. I was better, but he had continued to take drugs and could scarcely pilot—we missed the landing strip at Santa Monica Airport twice in the fog. That is when I, who knew nothing about flying an airplane, became the copilot at his rather blitzed request. Reading gauges that made absolutely no sense to me, we finally landed successfully on the third attempt.

Back home, safe with my children, this experience left me deeply shaken, the beliefs about myself and the direction of my life in turmoil. How had I gone the wrong way when I had left Michel to go the right way? I truly didn't know—and so it was that on August 14, 1980, a date easily recalled because it coincides with a friend's birthday, I literally raised my arms to heaven in the kitchen of my apartment in Los Angeles and, in effect, gave up the failing ways of the ego to God: "I will do whatever You want."

It was only "in effect," however, because had the surrender been complete, believe me, there would have been no need for a whopper of a second near-death later on.

7

The Return of Divine Mother

One month later that little vote of confidence in Someone Up There brought into my life a wonderful woman named Pia Dunne. She taught meditation, dream interpretation and past-life recall, recommending their content be written down because, "Some day these first steps will be very precious to you." I had kept diaries and journals since childhood, but by faithfully extending her advice over the years, I have access now to hundreds of dreams and meditations as accurate as when they occurred. Those included in this book, then, are true to their time—like this dream from January 6, 1981 heralding the return of Divine Mother.

> I was in a hotel complex. There were several bassinets joined together and I was delighted to see a baby in at least one of them. A dark-haired woman came immediately and picked up the baby. She was the mother. She stood in front of a source of background light, her face slightly shadowed because of it. She was extremely psychic, talking about people in my life by name.
> I looked at a man near us and said something like, "My, God! She's really god!"
> *[I had meant to write "good" at the end of that sen-*

tence, but unconsciously substituted the correct word.]

She said there was a Frenchman in my life. I said yes, but She had no interest in him. I asked her some questions, the most pressing about the book, particularly how I would be able to finish it. "A man with a beard," was the answer. He was important to my life, involved with the book in some capacity and would support it. I don't think there was a time limit on his involvement, though.

This was an inspiration [in-spirit] dream. It gives me a lot of hope and encouragement.

That dream not only re-introduced Divine Mother to me, but three months later I met the man who definitely had a beard at the time, Alex Tegmen. The book he helped come to fruition as a participant in the story, as you will see, was not the book I was working on then, but this one about Her.

The next week, Pia asked if I would question Divine Mother on her behalf regarding a personal matter in need of resolution. I knew Pia had contact with Divine Mother, often referring to Her as the "female side of God." Not knowing any more about Her, however, and not yet having realized that the woman in the dream, Madre in my childhood, and Divine Mother were one and the same, I didn't feel up to it. Pia just smiled at my protest, saying, "You can do it."

And so it was, on the evening of January 15, 1981, after putting Ty and Linc to bed, I closed my eyes, went into meditation and saw: nothing. Not knowing what else to do, I telepathically asked this blankness if I could please speak with Divine Mother.

Still nothing happened, until out of the darkness a lantern of light appeared ... and then the woman who held it out in front of Her. She led the way for the children following along behind Her, mine included. She was the most beautiful blend of East and West, in a white wedding dress with a white mantilla over her head. She walked into the sunlight and my children were with Her.

She said, "I don't want to talk about Pia. I want to talk about your children."

She sat down on a bench in the park and removed the mantilla because it was hot. She has light brown hair, long, with rolling waves like the ocean. I could not see Her face well; it wouldn't distinguish, and there was so much light I almost lost Her altogether. She had Ty and Linc by Her side.

"Ty is very special," She said. "He adores you and needs to be adored." She is not as concerned with Linc, but I felt She was in love with both my children; She only had eyes and ears for them.

She said: "Ty is the moon, Linc is the sun. Together they can light up your universe. They need to be shown the one in the other and develop that. That is what they are here for."

[Linc needed to become more reflective like Ty and the moon, while Ty needed to become more outgoing like Linc and the sun.]

She said I can show them how to do that, and that She often brings them to this park. She is really watching over them.

Only then did She discuss Pia's concern.

Several days later I read the meditation aloud to Pia. Her eyes widened as she listened and then she put one hand over her mouth in awe because no one knew she had looked at each of her three children in turn when they were little and said, echoing Divine Mother's words to me about my children, "You are the sun, you are the moon, you are the stars, and together you light up my world."

We knew then that I had indeed spoken with Divine Mother and very shortly thereafter, my heavenly triune of Ty as the moon and Linc as the sun became complete on earth with Alex: if you search the constellation of Cancer, you'll find his last name is the same as one of its stars.

A Past Life

Many dreams described Alex immediately prior to meeting him. I was told about his life in precise detail, even down to his preference in soap brands. This certainly contributed to powerful recognition at first sight; I couldn't miss him. The reaction was mutual. Friends who witnessed our first meeting at a party saw his double-take as I walked into the room. Years later he told me the double-take was because he thought he knew me and, as you will see by the end of this section, he did.

While there was an intense, immediate and abiding bond between us, only I experienced a concurrent sense of fear and danger. Knowing intuitively that Alex had personal power of some kind, definitely the power to change me, I attributed my unease to that, but my alarm to this:

Once, early on, I had walked past Alex in a darkened room and saw his whole face transformed by a supernatural light just then visible and visibly connecting us. His face receded into the darkness, like a slate-grey easel on which the light superimposed an illuminated series of different faces, those of his past lives. I stopped dead still, told him not to move, and watched as face after face materialized and then disappeared.

In retrospect, Divine Mother had manifested this experience, but it was as frightening as it was exhilarating—what *had* I gotten into here? And why couldn't I feel calm with Alex until I saw a particular face *beneath* the beard he had then, a face which had *not* been included among the many that night? That was his real face somehow, one I recognized strongly, but why was it so familiar, comforting and safe?

To begin answering my questions, the dreams took a sudden turn into a completely different time frame. For example, there was a large 19th-century home with a wooden exterior in the dreams; a very specific, early Victorian living room furnished in the detailed dark wood and design of the period; raised rectangles of dirt whose meaning and purpose were indecipherable to me; lilies of the valley; and lilacs, which Alex and I, independently, have always loved.

Pia was working with me on interpreting dreams, and I still marvel how Divine Mother placed a clairvoyant in my life to make sure the powerful dreams She now sent would be investigated in detail and that I would learn much about dream interpretation from it. One day Pia asked about this particular historical period appearing in my dreams: did I have a personal connection to it?

I told her a psychic I had met a few years earlier at a party, not someone to whom I had gone for a reading, said in a past life I was Fanny Appleton, wife of the 19th-century poet, Henry Longfellow. I had never heard of her.

Pia thought that lifetime was coming up now in the dreams, but I disavowed the idea of having been married to a famous man. It seemed like something disreputable psychics might say to gratify the ego of the person in front of them. Why wasn't I, say, Sally Smith, wife of nondescript Bill, buried in an avalanche and never heard from again?

Pia said with conviction, "It doesn't matter how the information came to you. If you're supposed to know, you'll be told. I think you should look into it."

The dreams had never let me down and eventually evoked enough interest to send me to the UCLA library in search of information. I found a collection of Fanny Appleton's journals and letters entitled *Mrs. Longfellow*. I began reading and was soon on the edge of my seat, *knowing in advance* of the next page what would be on it, from where she went and whom she knew to details like the many *lilacs* she had planted in front of their home.

It was so powerful that I literally had to shut the book after each encounter with a memory and recompose myself before continuing, I remember, because the same thing has happened now reviewing it for this chapter. I hadn't read it again because my life was in progress; I didn't want it to be influenced or guided by what had happened to her. On the contrary, I wanted conditions, events and relationships to develop on their own; then, someday, I could look back to see if the similarities had continued. But that has made going into her life *now*, which of course included her marriage with Henry, all the more shocking. The facts of their lives, individually or combined, are so similar to Alex and me, they literally make me light-headed with recognition.

Fortunately, I xeroxed a copy of the book so as never to lose the penciled notes I had written on the margin of one page in anticipation of information on the next, before erasing them and returning the book to the library. It was the only evidence then of what I knew to be true before reading it, a personally valuable property for anyone suddenly on the trail of something big: reincarnation. (See Appendix B)

Details of a past life resonate with reality for the individual involved, just as the after-death visit by my grandfather resonated with truth for me. Recognition of a past life generally requires this inner knowing, but it isn't objective proof, nor is it measurable. But adding up the similarities between the two lives *is measurable* and, while I can't prove the past life as Fanny one hundred percent, I can present correlations so compelling as to have made a believer of me.

Fanny possessed remarkable self-assurance, the kind of confidence I had mysteriously assumed in my childhood as a facade to shield the Golden Girl, but may certainly have dug out of the closet of my own past life as this woman. It was a dignity that people often mistook, even in my early teens, for good breeding and an affluent background. I did not have that at all, but Fanny did. She grew up on Boston's Beacon Hill in a home of substantial wealth.

Now, in regard to Beacon Hill, there is a connection that had little meaning to me when it occurred. In August 1969, one month before I went to Vassar and a few weeks after my dream about the Wayside Inn, a boyfriend attending Harvard Business School invited me to stay with him. I had never before been on the East Coast, yet this first trip there took me right from Logan Airport to where he was living that summer: Beacon Hill. I went directly to Fanny's old

Longfellow's Wayside Inn; Sudbury, Massachusetts.
As dreamed by the author in 1969, five years before first seeing it on May 18, 1974. Two days later she learned the Inn had been built by one of her own relatives, David Howe, in the 1700's. Later still she learned of her many connections to the Longfellows.

The Grist Mill, Longfellow's Wayside Inn.
A replica of David Howe's mill, not far from the original 1740's site. The rustic surroundings were first seen by the author from the back of a buckboard in her 1969 dream.

The Old Kitchen, Longfellow's Wayside Inn.
Exactly as the author dreamed it in 1969, five years prior to first seeing it on May 18, 1974. The oven is located to the immediate left of the hearth; it is built into the brick fireplace, just as it was in the dream.

Across the road from Longfellow's Wayside Inn.
The meadow, the buckboard, and the hills that change from green to pink in the autumn, seen first in the 1969 dream and then in fact on May 18, 1974. "Wendy, you don't look like yourself anymore."

Longfellow House: 105 Brattle Street, Cambridge, Massachusetts.
The 19th century home of Henry and Fanny Appleton Longfellow throughout their marriage. (Her funeral was held on their 18th wedding anniversary, July 13, 1861.) The house was dreamed about by the author a few months prior to first seeing it in May, 1981. The lilacs in the foreground, also in the dream, were planted by Fanny 150 years ago.

The Library, Longfellow House, Cambridge.
The room in which Fanny's dress caught fire on July 7, 1861. The room, furniture
and decor were dreamed about by the author a few months prior to first seeing them
in May, 1981.

A marble bust of Fanny by Lorenzo Bartolini.

The author in 1970, remarkably resembling Fanny.

Fanny (Frances) Appleton Longfellow (1817-1861) from a painting by G.P.A. Healy.

The author in 1970 and in a pose unintentionally similar to Fanny's.
This photograph was taken seven years before the author even knew of Fanny's
existence. The striking facial similarities between the two women are one of many
significant factors bolstering the belief in reincarnation.

The bust of Fanny with photographs of the author (1970–1977), further emphasizing their similar features.

The Longfellow sons, Charles and Ernest, with the author's sons, Ty (upper left), and Linc (upper right). A virtually identical resemblance between the two sets of children.

The author and a bust of Henry Longfellow (1807-1882), at Longfellow's Wayside Inn, May, 1981.

street without knowing it. A month later, a California friend visited at Vassar and wanted to see Cambridge. Once there, we needed a place to spend the night. My friend chose an inn on Brattle Street, which turned out to be the same street on which Fanny and Henry had lived their entire married life. I did not decide to be on either Beacon Hill or Brattle Street, nor visit them in the order Fanny had lived on them, yet Divine Mother ensured that happened. And the timing (right after the Wayside Inn dream, as well as one location after the other) became very meaningful, as you will understand by the end of this chapter.

While the Appletons lived in Boston, they originally came from England the same time as my family of descent, the Leavitts, and were as devoted to genealogy as I am. Fanny's father enjoyed speaking French, entered into business which often took him to Paris, and was strict, although not as severe as my father. Fanny also lost her mother early in life, spent extended time in Europe and attended private school. She became deeply interested in spirituality and the Transcendentalists of the time; Thoreau and Emerson lived nearby, and one of her teachers was a Transcendentalist.

Fanny was an intellectual woman with a lovely sense of humor, who, poor thing, had to learn French, too, but I don't think that ever took place in an attic. She maintained personal journals very similar to mine, was an equally copious writer of letters, and kept diaries of her children's lives which I was meticulous in keeping as well.

Fanny was tall and so am I, we look alike, and our two sons have virtually identical faces. As Henry was older than Fanny, so Alex is older than I. Henry and Alex have similar features, characteristics, habits, and professions; and, as was written about Henry, Alex obviously has a soul "which has an affinity with the light." I absolutely believe they are the same person—and so does he. In fact, when Alex discussed the double-take at our first meeting, thinking that he knew me, he added, "I was recognizing Fanny, and that was the beginning of Fanny and Henry this lifetime..."

According Divine Mother, Alex and I agreed before our births to rectify the errors of that lifetime in this one and bring it forward in a comprehensible and public format in order to help enlighten the West about karma and reincarnation.

Now, in regard to karma and reincarnation overall, the Appletons, Leavitts, and Howes lived within a short radius of each other at a time when few ships had crossed the Atlantic to the New World. That made me wonder, "What if I am actually related to Fanny Appleton this lifetime?" It was a heady thought, one which would confirm the idea we are reborn into our own genetic line. I decided to find out and learned from 200 hours of research that it is true to a staggering degree:

Fanny and I share direct lineage from the kings and queens of the Franks as far back as 20 a.d. to the kings and queens of the Swedes in 217 a.d.; from the last indigenous Prince and Princess of Wales to Princess Diana. Direct descendency continues from Charlemagne, Louis I of France, the English barons as well as King John of the Magna Carta, and his parents, Eleanor of Acquitaine and Henry II, the king who had Becket killed in Canterbury, a neighboring town extremely meaningful to me in boarding school for this very story when I had no idea why it affected me deeply.

There is documentation for scores of shared English and European ancestors of equal rank, but none of the royal roots are as significant as the route their genes took during the 16th and 17th century in, near and around Ashford, Kent, England, where the school is located. Fanny's part of the family lived so near my part of the family, they must have have tripped over each other in adjoining cow fields.

But they did more than that. During the same centuries, the genes were traveling right into my English great-grandfather long ago, Thomas Dudley. He was the second governor of Massachusetts, the blood relative of Fanny, and the Ipswich, Massachusetts neighbor for four years of Samuel Appleton, Fanny's English great-grandfather long ago.

The Appleton line, part of mine, had traveled into the same American state and town; two of my relatives, the Rogers, even delivered the eulogies at Appleton's funeral.

A total of five 17th-century marriages in Massachusetts link the two families. (See Appendix A-2) One marriage unbelievably occurred in Marshfield, where I lived as well; another ties Fanny to the Howes of the Wayside Inn, and still another ties the Appleton/Dudleys to the Howe/Leavitts, uniting all four families. (Even Longfellow fits as a descendent of John Paybody, the great-grandfather of *David Howe's wife*. This link to the Howe descendents tied Longfellow to the Appletons independently of Fanny and it ties him to *me*: I also descend from John Paybody.)

All in all, hundreds of direct-line connections uniting Fanny and me weave in and out of time and place to create a remarkable tapestry of genalogical material as if it were a comforter of good will from the past to cover me and cover you with the knowledge that yes, we do reincarnate into our own genetic line; yes, we frequently were our own ancestors.

Now, information of a completely different kind also binds Fanny and me. One July day in 1861, Fanny was using matches to melt sealing wax to close an envelope containing locks of her children's hair. She accidentally caught her long, hooped dress on fire and burned to death. Henry's efforts to extinguish the fire resulted in burns to his face and he grew a beard, like Alex had, to cover the scars. Fanny did not live to see the beard—and *that* is why it was difficult for me to feel comfortable with Alex until I could see his "real" face beneath his beard; it was Henry's face all along.

The way Fanny died was extremely meaningful to me because absolutely no one knew about all the fires in my life or how often I have actually *been on fire*.

When I was about four, my grandfather was burning weeds in our large vacant back lot, a legal activity in Southern California at the time. The fire got out of control, forced him into a corner of the chain-link fence around the yard, and trapped him. Grandpa yelled to me, "Get help! Get Mr.

Kirsch next door!"

My heart pounding, "Grandpa's going to die, he's going to die," I ran next door as fast as I could, told Mr. Kirsch what had happened, and watched in agony while he casually finished writing a letter, licked the envelope, addressd it and stamped it. Only then did he call the fire department. Fortunately, they arrived in time to put out the fire and relieve Grandpa from his perch high on the fence where he had retreated, he said, "like a monkey."

Not long after this, Grandma, Grandpa and I drove to Farmer John's to drop Grandpa off for his night job as a watchman—and we saw a huge fire in the slaughterhouse. Grandpa got out of the car and walked right into the burning building. Soon after he disappeared, fire engines roared into the drive, and I burst into tears on Grandma's lap, crying "He's going to die!"

Grandpa came back later and put his head in through the open window to let us know the fire was under control. Grandma said, "Wendy was afraid you would die." He then reached into the car, patted my arm, and whispered what he later proved from the other side, "Grandpa's don't ever die."

The first instance of my being on fire took place in France. I had been boiling water for tea, turned my back to the stove to chat with the au pere and had no idea why she suddenly lunged at me, beating on my back, but my blouse had caught fire from the gas flame. I don't know what would have happened without her; no one else was home.

The second occurred at the home of friends in England during a cold mid-term break from boarding school. They had given me an old heating pad to use with the warning not to go to sleep on it. The instructions were carefully followed, but I turned it on "for a second" in the night and fell back to sleep. Tremendous heat caused me to awaken and jump up. When I did, the pad ignited, as did my nightwear and the bedding. Somehow I got out of my clothes, but then I couldn't unplug the pad from the wall socket; the solid mahogany bed, too heavy for me even to budge, stood in front of it. The daughter of the household, also my age, happened to be coming up the stairs. Empowered with the superhuman strength of wanting to save her home, she managed to move the massive bed and pull the plug from the socket. We stamped out the flames, and what we could not put out, we threw out the window, accidentally catching the curtains and wallpaper on fire. We beat on the fire devouring the wallpaper, yanked down the heavy curtains and threw them out the window, too.

The third occurred in England as well, during a college break when I was visiting a very dear friend in London, named, I swear, *Fanny*. She was in nurse's training and had gone off early, leaving me to sleep. It was freezing cold in the flat and on awakening, I couldn't find a heater. I went in the kitchen, closed the door and window to keep out the draft, and then turned on all the stove burners for warmth. Well, I turned five knobs but there were only four burners; what had I actually done? I opened the oven door to find out—and the gas ignited in my face.

The oven pilot had gone out. When I turned the fifth knob, for the oven, and opened the oven door, the accumulated gas escaped. Without ventilation in the room, the gas ignited instantly from the four burners. I lost the hair above my forehead, my eyebrows and eyelashes, and was taken to the hospital for second-degree burns under my eyes.

There was a fourth incident years later in my Los Angeles apartment involving a very old lamp. All I did was *touch* the shade and the lamp started smoking. I immediately switched off the breakers. The smoking died down, but when I turned the breakers back on, the fire came alive and traveled down the wire, behind the couch, onto an extension cord running the length of the couch, catching it on fire, and then up a wooden bookcase, catching that on fire, too. Neighbors came to my assistance and we put out the fire just as the fire department arrived. I wasn't close to being hurt. That was significant because the fire occurred in 1989, after I knew about Fanny Appleton and just after the second near-death which heralded the rapid decline of negative karma in my life—as the following event, so full of symbolism, marks what I hope is the end of fires once and for all.

As it happened, several years ago I went downstairs for some reason and noticed a fire in the apartment building dumpster. I ran back in to call 911 and alert Alex. He went out to pull the dumpster from *beneath* one of the apartments which otherwise would have gone up in flames, taking the rest of the building with it. When I went back to make sure Alex was all right, he had a fire extinguisher. We removed the pin together and then I held the lever down while he directed the hose toward the fire. Together, he and I, Fanny and Henry, *finally* handled a fire correctly until the fire department arrived to put it out entirely.

Now, there are aspects of my life which do not perfectly coincide with Fanny's. The dissimilarities I found had either been resolved in her lifetime and didn't need a second airing in this one or were brought up from past lives other than the one as Fanny to be dealt with now, in my lifetime. Fanny lost her mother early through death, for example, not mental illness, but *why* I didn't lose my mother the same way is explained by Divine Mother in a later chapter of this book.

Fanny Appleton was obviously important to pursue and I was fortunate that year to make a trip to Cambridge, Massachusetts, where the Longfellow House is located. Of course it proved to be the wooden home of my dreams, full of their 19th-century, Victorian furniture; the lilacs Fanny planted over a hundred years ago had grown up like trees in the front, and lilies of the valley clustered near the side door. The lilies of the valley weren't necessarily from the last century like the lilacs, but they had definitely appeared in my dreams as a signpost, a connector between the dreams and this specific place. They also symbolize a marriage, an initiation into spiritual abilities, and something that was yet to occur.

The home is now an historic landmark, open to the

public, exquisitely preserved and, because of that, easily remembered when I saw it again; nothing had changed in 138 years, just as nothing has changed now in 156 years. Too often a McDonald's or shopping mall stands on the grounds of one of our beloved old homesteads, making recognition virtually impossible when most of us do need some kind of visual cue to trigger recall of the past or to confirm it.

I was so transported by the place that I dared confide to the guide at the door, a dear older gentleman, "I think I was Fanny Appleton in another life." People have burned at the stake in Massachusetts for saying less than that, but he looked in my eyes and nodded in recognition, saying, "You look just like her." I was then graciously invited in, taken on a personal tour of the house and, without being told, picked out the room in which Fanny had died.

He introduced me to another guide, a young woman, and explained my story. She didn't even flinch, but nodded in recognition, too, and asked if I would like to see Fanny's personal, hand-written journals, letters and papers; they were up on a floor not open to the public. I went upstairs, was trusted to sit alone with these most intimate of Fanny's records, and cried because there was no question in my mind that this woman and I were one; I *knew* her.

I knew, too, a particular detail only Fanny could have known for sure—she didn't catch herself on fire. One letter among the many in my hands that day, from a relative or neighbor, verified what I knew to be true: the children had been playing with the matches on the floor at Fanny's feet and *that* is how her hoop skirt caught fire. My recollection from the letter is that this was withheld from public knowledge in order to protect the children during their lifetime.

Two other, very personal things which had not made any sense in my life before knowing about Fanny came to mind during this trip—and made total sense. As a very little girl I had adored Abraham Lincoln, to an extent beyond the capacity of a child to feel. At about the age of 9, I was alone, happily watching a television program about his life. No one had told me he had been assassinated. When that information came on, I went into the bathroom and burst into tears that a wonderful man whom I loved so much had died, and died that way. It was devastating to me when it should not have been to one so young ... but Fanny loved Lincoln, had "great hopes in Lincoln," as "just the man for the hour." She put her faith in him to pull the country through the Civil War, knew "there are no doubt wretches [ ] who would glory in an assassination," and was relieved one didn't happen. She just did not live long enough to know he was assassinated four years after she died.

The second thing to make sense was this: I had been taught as a very little girl by my grandmother to pray, "Now I lay me down to sleep, I pray the Lord my soul to keep. If I should die before I wake, I pray the Lord my soul to take," and I had repeated it faithfully throughout my childhood and then some ... but *always* adding what Fanny would have known to add, "And please, dear God, no wars or fires."

After so many discoveries at the Longfellow house, a girlfriend who was also visiting the East Coast met me there that afternoon as planned. We took pictures outside and, viewing me through the camera lens, she said, just like the photographer at the Wayside Inn years before, "You don't look like yourself."

I laughed and said, "I know." This time, however, I knew exactly who I was.

The next day a friend from Vassar with whom I was staying in Cambridge drove me to the Wayside Inn. She is Ty's godmother and the first person I called after finding the genealogical tie to the Wayside Inn through David Howe at the Boston Public Library years earlier. Involved in the sage from its inception, she wanted to see where it had originally begun. Well, not only did we find a fresh bouquet of *lilies of the valley* in a vase at the front desk, linking the dreams of the lilies to the Longfellow house *and* to the Wayside Inn, but remember those raised rectangles of dirt in the dreams? *They were there*: raised beds, raked and ready for planting a vegetable or flower garden.

I really had to laugh then as everything fell into place. One of the most well-known writings of Henry Longfellow, Fanny's husband and mine, is *"Tales of the Wayside Inn."* Because of that collection of narrative poems bearing its name, the place I had dreamed about so many years earlier without a hint of any connection to it, is today called *"Longfellow's Wayside Inn."*

8

At the Inner Altar

The work with Pia finished at the end of a year on the assumption it was possible to follow Divine Mother on my own. It may have been my assumption, actually, when I was still just a babe in the woods of spirituality and could scarcely see the forest for the trees. As it turned out, however, Divine Mother had conveniently placed Her park bench in a clearing right next to a literal forest in Divine Meditation, all ready to begin new learning with me.

Earlier, a group of us had meditated with Pia to find a spontaneous animal image; it would represent our inner nature and how we relate to the world. In my meditation, a newborn fawn appeared in a mist of golden lavender light, the color of spiritual third-eye sight. Getting up for the first time on shaking legs, she was as unaccustomed to standing on them as I was on my new spiritual legs. That is why the scene Divine Mother created above was so perfect: the forest and the clearing are a deer's natural habitat—the ideal place for me and my inner fawn to gain strength and grow.

Divine Mother and I spent many meditations in that scene, one which turned out to be a pun on another kind of clearing: clearing out the debris of the past. A variety of puns were learned here, such as how "clearing" also means a place to see clearly, or how a nearby field, filling naturally with assorted images, represents our own "field of vision." One funny pun was a locomotive shooting through my field in response to something I had wondered about doing; it meant the "motive" behind the idea was "loco."

Since images, like these, are received consciously, we can easily interpret their meaning, experience their impact as intended, and ask for an explanation if they are confusing—none of which happens in the dream state. When Divine Meditation becomes a regular routine, dreaming tapers off substantially because its purpose of communication is being met in this far more effective and direct way.

There is, of course, a garden in Divine Meditation, and we can grow anything. For instance, I could plant coins, a pun on "change" in our lives, and watch them grow into a tree laden with the buds of a better relationship, happier children, miracles. All of the plantings, like prayers, came to fruition over time. Unlike prayer, however, these inner actions are not just requests; they involve one's whole mind in partnership with Divine Mother God in the natural process of creation.

Using other symbolism, I might dig in the garden with a shovel and make an accidental find of gold pieces buried in the ground; they represent our own fully developed soul power which, in my case and as you can see, had not yet been acknowledged. It was then possible to read on the back of the shovel, a physical tool, the psychological or emotional "tool" necessary to access the soul power in daily life.

These are just examples, but by using the concept of planting with Divine Mother, we can grow, cultivate, and harvest knowledge and foreknowledge, accomplishments, abilities, good relationships, health, a harmonious work environment, peaceful family life, spiritual awareness, help for others who are dear to us, or assistance for those in the news whose situations cause deep concern, from the 1999 Littleton school shootings to events in our own neighborhood.

We really can do something by coming here to plant

our good intentions for ourselves, for others, and for the world. The soil is our soul, the seeds our thoughts, desires and hopes. The sunlight is the energy of God, the water our love. That is all it takes to create with Divine Mother. And this is undoubtedly why, when we made the mistake long ago of projecting Her entirely outside of ourselves as myth or matter or anything other than light, She became known as Mother Earth and Mother Nature.

Because this process is done with Her, it is different from ordering what we want through affirmations or visualization. These means are not as effective or fast as we would like for two very valid, unrecognized reasons:

1) The truth inherent in an affirmation or visualization *already exists in us*, but the ego lies between the two like filling in a sandwich: truth/ego/truth. The applied truth cannot connect with the interior truth any more than one piece of bread can lie flat against another with a slab of salami in the middle. Without uniform contact, the ego pops up like the salami, protesting that the truth is a lie; we believe the ego and ironically reinforce what we were trying to change.

2) Order on demand worked before we accumulated any negative karma to stand in the way of *having* what we want. That creates a sandwich, too: truth/karma/truth. A lot of hefty "spade" work must be done in the garden of Divine Meditation to clear the way for the arrival of our heart's desires outside of it, because God never denies our wishes; we have just blocked the avenues to their manifestation.

When we decide on something we want, the path to it is not arbitrary, the shortest distance between two points, or as the crow flies. It is strictly determined and mapped out by our own karma—by all our positive or negative thoughts, words and actions in the past relating to that objective.

Along the road of life, negative karma comes in the form of obstacles, detours and ruts we have put in place ourselves, in times past, when we did not care about the consequences or did not realize there would be any. Once the goal has been set, however, they come up again to give us the opportunity to do what we didn't do before: handle them correctly by resolving them *in* the light and then allow them to be dissolved *by* the light. As this occurs, we realize how often true learning is a matter of *unlearning* the errors of the past.

Now, as we continue on the road of life, our positive karma comes up, too, making the way so deceptively easy at times that suddenly finding our car upside down in a ditch because we didn't see a karmic roadblock before we ran into it can be a nasty surprise. It may make us doubt our course, our direction, or even the goal itself, when problems only arise to show us *what we need to correct in order to reach our goal.* As soon as the corrections are made, the roadblock vanishes like a mirage, we're upright again and free to travel on.

Once, on the rocky road to financial recovery, a block wall had been built in Divine Meditation in front of a row of crisp one hundred dollar bills. I then had to work on that wall with Divine Mother, sometimes taking it apart brick by emotional or psychological brick, to understand how and why it had become constructed against my financial well-being. There were many detours on the road to solvency because money was tied to so many other issues in my life.

When our desire manifests in a lasting manner is primarily contingent on the time it takes to remove the blocks. Sometimes Divine Mother gives a specific date, but just as often the answer is "soon" (which in eternal terms bears no resemblance to "soon" on planet earth). As a consequence, I disregard the time element and ask instead, "What is the lesson?" and get to it quickly, because unless there are severe astrological constraints, timing is greatly determined by how long we linger over learning. Once done, it can still seem as if what we want is never going to grow in our garden, or we experience a partial return on our investment in an entire packet of seeds. Getting only part or an inadequate version of what we want is not a sign of failure, but a postcard from God saying our goal is on its way. That is the time to go back and add a side-dressing of faith, not run for the nearest Roto-tiller to start planting all over again.

When the *reasons behind a problem* are handled with Divine Mother—something we will be exploring "soon"—a successful outcome is guaranteed because She always gets to the root of the problem. Since we are dealing directly with the unconscious, there is no need to "leave it to the unconscious" to manifest as is taught in regard to visualization or affirmations. Instead, we are able to observe and participate in a process with Divine Mother that is otherwise hidden from view and that *substantially* hastens a fulfilled life.

Another valuable reason for learning the meaning of symbols in Divine Meditation is that the meaning is identical in dreams, thus making dreams easier to interpret. In addition, and very importantly, the meaning can be applied to the outer world or to our immediate environment. Once, for example, I found ten pennies and a button in a water fountain. They symbolized my being emotionally (water) protected (button) by Divine Mother (fountain) during many upcoming changes (pennies)—and I was.

For a more detailed example on a world level, let's pretend we are unaware of the significance of a car crash in a Paris tunnel in August, 1997, and can read *only* the symbolism surrounding it. First, a tunnel represents death and rebirth; a car, which means a life, crashed inside the tunnel, so at least one person died. This is affirmed by the fact that above the tunnel is the Pont de l'Alma, which means "bridge of the soul." Further, the road going into the tunnel parallels the Seine River. A river indicates the stream of consciousness continuing throughout life *and* death; since "Seine" means a fishing net, which Christ used allegorically as a fisher of men, this is someone who lived a parallel life by drawing people to them, to love and/or to goodness in both life and death in order to open their hearts. The tunnel is near Notre Dame (Our Lady), so the person was literally a Lady and/or a woman functioning in a divine capacity. Verifying this, La Flamme de la Liberté—a huge sculpted gold flame representing freedom—stands on top of the Pont de l'Alma directly above the accident. Because Alma (soul), the flame

(Divine Mother), Liberté (freedom), gold (enlightenment) and Paris (the city of light) converge here, the soul was very evolved, luminous, deeply connected to Divine Mother and emancipated into the light after death. She was taken to Pitié-Salpêtrière Hospital whose name and original intent to help those in need indicate she was compassionate (Pitié) to humanity and/or humanity to her; and she was involved with saltpeter (Salpêtrière) used to make explosives. To preserve her anonymity, and confirming that this was a woman and a Lady as earlier surmised, she received the name of the saint of the day, St. Patricia, meaning "of patrician or noble birth." By definition, a saint is a patron or sponsor of great benevolence, so the woman must have been very charitable and/or occupied with charities. Lastly, St. Patricia was born into the aristocracy, broke away from a marriage with royalty, gave substantially to the poor and died young.

All in all, doesn't this perfectly describe the life and death of Diana, Princess of Wales?

A different example of reading the symbolism outside of meditation occurred a few years ago when a friend and I went to the old Getty Museum in Malibu. We stood on the balcony, enjoying the ocean view in the distance, absent-mindedly watching planes fly over the water; they had long ribbons of advertisements attached to their tails, too far away for us to read. My friend was concerned about a problem and knew the answer, but found it hard to act on and wanted advice. I said, "Divine Mother would tell you, 'Just do it.'" She nodded, but was still reluctant. We walked down to the beach then and, as we did, one of the airplanes with a long ribbon tail buzzed by and caught our attention. It was advertising a new Frank Sinatra album, "Just Duet."

Another way of translating the learning within to the outside world is a little different. If I saw myself putting on make-up in a meditation, that could mean I looked awful and needed it; I should "make-up with someone;" I was "making-up" something, or, remembering the inclusive nature of symbols in dreams, Divine Meditation and the universe itself, all three. By way of another example, after Ty went to college and we had missed a weekly phone call or two, I wanted to know how he was doing and went to my inner garden to find out. There he was, busily planting seeds of some kind. When he stood back, I saw the seeds sprout into chaise lounges. Odd as that might be, it was a perfectly appropriate symbol because it turned out he had taken time off and was just resting.

The symbolism developed over time, but the basic concept remained the same—and it was always as fun as it was fascinating to learn that the universe constantly speaks to us and it is more than possible to know what it is saying.

Often, too, time was spent just resting next to Divine Mother, Her arms lovingly around me. She was, as She is, a beautiful prism of light and color in the form of a woman, changing over in this period from the white wedding dress to a soft pink sari. Sometimes it was difficult to focus on the finer features of Her face or the exact color of Her eyes, but it was always easy to find peace with Her.

I was also reunited in these meditations with certain people, as you will be. Along with Divine Mother's participation and guidance, we would all talk together, working through past and present events in our lives until the common link of love was reached again. Loving more was a major theme in these early days and I embraced it, happy to learn that no matter what is perceived in the world, we really do all love each other.

Christ, a friend, very often came to lend a hand in the light. He had, in fact, been in the meditations from the very beginning and spoke as readily as Divine Mother. He was a spiritual guide in His own right, but always adjunct to Her. Once, not knowing the answer at all, I asked Him what my mission was. He pointed to the sky. It darkened into night. The stars came out to dance about before stopping to form one simple sentence of light, "Write for God."

There were a number of other "scenes" in which the truth could be "seen." One was a cottage located near a field of roses by the garden and clearing. Alex often stood at the door wearing a white suit. He rarely came in, but seemed to be making sure everything was all right. Once I noticed a bassinet near the window. In it was a sleeping baby girl. Divine Mother said she was a part of me and that we were taking care of her here until she was grown.

Divine Mother would invariably sit in a comfortable, over-stuffed chair by the cottage fireplace during these meditations and write words of wisdom in the fire for me to read from the double-bed in which I lay a few feet away, recovering, I think, from my life. This was the first time words appeared in the meditations. Also, although I didn't know it then, a fire—like the flame in Paris just mentioned—is one of Her symbols. Fire is not only light, but in its wake there is always room for fresh, abundant new growth.

The sheets and spread on the double-bed were peach, the color of restoration. Several dreams at this time took place in restaurants, a French word which literally means "restoration." Despite my aversion, having learned French certainly had its merits when it came to understanding some of the symbolism. I often kept a French and English dictionary nearby, and still do, but for another reason: the images and words are so specifically selected by Divine Mother that often only their original derivation reveals Her exact intent.

Later on, there was a log cabin and, inside, a movie screen on which were projected some of my past lives from start to finish in order to learn from them. Outside the cabin, Divine Mother and I would sit in Adirondack chairs on the deck and talk while my children played. I always appeared spontaneously in a red-checked dress, one I loved as a young mother. Divine Mother inevitably had a notebook with Her from which She would refer to upcoming events and lessons in my life—and I would laugh when the notepaper scattered with the wind as naturally as it can in life.

I don't know why She never switched to a computer, but I do know that something later made me feel just like Her with that notebook. It is an event worth mentioning here in detail, because along with facilitating our enlightenment, Divine Mother ensures our protection, too. In July, 1993, my son Ty, his girlfriend and I went to Magic Mountain for a day of fun. Standing in line for a ride, however, I began to be hit by waves of violently disruptive energy, so much so that I asked Divine Mother then and there what was wrong. She said something was going to happen, but it would be easier to talk with Her that night at home. I did, and She informed me there would be a 6.7 earthquake.

That made me quake a bit, actually, the seismic numbers were so precise. I was not given the date, nor was I told that people would die. Instead, Divine Mother said that the greatest overall damage would be the intensification of fear for those living in Los Angeles. I was allowed to tell my sons, Alex and a very few specified friends about it, but no one else, because the denial against anyone being able to predict an earthquake, and against one really happening, was so ingrained it would not be believed.

In the end, even the people I told didn't take it that seriously until the earthquake suddenly hit six months later on January 17, 1994. The epicenter was in Northridge, very close to Magic Mountain where I had experienced the etheric foreshadowing. The afternoon of the quake, I ran around to friends in the apartment complex with my notebook in which the meditations warning of this event had been kept, saying, "Look at this, look at *this*!" Believing Divine Mother now, they started coming to my door wanting to know what else She had said.

Everyone agreed that the first seismic reading of 6.6 was close enough. A few weeks later, however, the number was officially upgraded to Divine Mother's 6.7. I floated home on air after buying *The Los Angeles Times* with the 6.7 in print, exactly like the pages in my notebook. Still, it did feel a bit like being in a science-fiction movie. "Weird woman has x-ray vision into the future!" That just could not happen in real life, but it did. There *is* a way we all can predict earthquakes, because Divine Mother will tell us what we need to know, *if we are only willing to hear Her.*

Divine Mother also provides a very calm assurance. No matter in what mood I might enter meditation during the early days of these spiritual endeavors—angry, anxious, or just inquisitive—I always left content and at ease. That was due in part to the relief of receiving needed information given about a particular problem, but always due in full to the experience of having reunited with Her.

Once, wanting to access on my own any as yet unremembered past lives, a library spontaneously appeared in Divine Meditation. The walls were lined with bookshelves, and one book in particular caught my attention. I removed it from the shelf, sat down in a comfortable chair in my mind and read, "There once was a man from Rome..." It was a past life about Alex, explaining the causes behind a current predicament with him. It was then I realized that past lives are not only recorded in images, but in the written word— which is how the phrase "to do a reading" may have originated.

From that point on, unless a scene could provide instruction in a more striking way, written words began to replace the images. Virtually everything is now written in Her golden light on the dark background of the skein of time and space while being simultaneously received telepathically. The telepathy could be enough, and often it is, but I am a writer, so seeing the words is more concrete and comfortable for me than just hearing them.

There were times when I would think that I was making up the words. That is a common misconception early in this work, but it is due to the simultaneous telepathy, of seeing and hearing at the same time, often in a voice similar to our own. To ease my apprehension, Divine Mother allotted one golden word at a time on the screen of my mind to minimize the chances of my correctly guessing an entire phrase before it was given.

Sometimes I still could guess a phrase correctly, so I asked Her to devise a way that would make it impossible for me to know what it was in advance of its completion. Divine Mother then kindly created a syntax and style *so* awkward no one could anticipate what was coming next. For example, She might say, "Of the canine take note, for on the wall constructed of wood in the garden a feline creature hurriedly is dashing," instead of, "Watch the dog, a cat's on the fence." This is obviously a more complicated approach, but it did help me believe Her, on occasion it still does, and it always makes me laugh.

In the beginning there were so many questions, problems and situations in need of resolution that I couldn't remember to bring them all up to Her in a meditative state. This was resolved with two tape-recorders. I recorded the questions on one, followed by a long pause. After rewinding, I turned on that recorder, as well as the second, and went into Divine Meditation. The second tape-recorder recorded the questions being played on the first *and*, in the pause left for them, my verbal answers as they were telepathically and/ or visually received.

Soon I became adept enough for casual conversation, the even flow of questions, answers, comments and scenes coming on its own. There is still so much information from Her now, however, that I can't retain it all without one tape-recorder. Using it also frees me to experience Her without having to worry at the same time about how to remember everything She is saying.

The tape-recorder is valuable for another reason. The information on the January 1994 earthquake, for example, was given by Divine Mother and recorded as She spoke in July, 1993 and again in August, 1993, so I know exactly how much in advance it was received. I try to transcribe all the tapes into notebooks or on the computer to have a copy for my records, but whenever possible I also save the tapes. They are one way of keeping the original dialogues with Her unedited and intact, as well as proving such information is real prophecy, not manufactured after the fact.

9

The Ego

If it's not nice to fool Mother Nature, it's *really* not nice to ignore what Divine Mother says, not because feigning deafness in the face of God is so futile considering Who's watching, but because it is so self-defeating. Divine Mother is an inner Oracle at Delphi. She does not mislead, and after all the pitfalls you're about to see me tumble into because it seemed so much easier to go my own way—right off a cliff—you'll know why it is *always* important to follow Her advice.

It started when the garden of my life suddenly didn't look right. What was that slithering past my pretty sweet peas and creeping through my clover?

Oh, yes. The ego.

Had I been a grown deer instead of a little fawn, I would have noticed it right away, strolled over and stepped on the worthless thing because in the end it would not leave without a life-and-death struggle to survive. That is not an overstatement. Since I didn't yet have the spiritual skills to combat such a cunning adversary, the ego believed it had the upper hand in a battle that literally would be waged to the death.

Despite claims by the Maytag repairman, the work with Divine Mother really had been the loneliest job in the world. No one completely understood my devotion to spirituality or my devotion to Her. My children were actually very interested in what Divine Mother had to say, but since their taste tended toward PacMan at the time, they weren't always in the room when I repeated it. Among those with whom I worked, God was at best an avocation, not a vocation; the calls they took were not from Divine Mother, but to close another deal. Alex got very busy with his own life and when Pia moved away, external support just stopped.

It was this isolation which allowed the ego to flourish in the underbrush, feeding on fear I had not yet conquered. Since fear manifests too, there were suddenly a lot of unwanted weeds coming up in my life. I didn't realize they had been planted by the ego because, frankly, this source of fear in all of us scared me the most. It would coil up in my mind taunting, "No one here has even heard of Divine Mother, so what makes you think that She's real or that you're going to write for God? You're going to end up like your mother because you don't have a good hoe, your rake is bent and— hey! Come back here!"

I did, often, because I believed that voice, too. Unlike Divine Mother's voice in meditation, however, this one outside of it *was* my voice, and it stemmed as much from fear as from stubbornness and doubt.

While stubbornness and doubt had held me in good stead by not allowing an entire collapse under the weight of my mother and father, they were deeply injurious and inappropriate now. We are supposed to flow along with the spiritual stream meandering through the garden of our soul, not stop to build a dam and then hole up in it like a beaver. Even so, that is exactly what I did. I did not want to let the ego go. It had stuck with me, not to mention to me, through thick and thin. I just didn't know then that without an ego there would be no thick or thin; there would be only the even balance of grace in between.

As it was, along with the sound now of a beaver gnawing nervously on its twigs, and the image of a fawn scared into the forest, Divine Mother must have looked at me for a long time like a few other animals we know: a bull with its head down, feet defiantly pushed into the ground; a dog jerking on its leash to go another way, and a horse She could lead to water but not make drink, because I wouldn't talk to Divine Mother until I was just bursting from the inordinate, ego-driven effort of staying away from Her.

Of course things went wrong. Instead of the continuous meditation that solves problems before they arise, I had turned things around, meditating only when the problems seemed beyond repair.

Despite profound meditations, dreams, and another woman coming into my life in 1985 with the Archangels for more clearing of the chakras, our spiritual energy centers, I still could not keep my identity straight—not with one ear open to the ego, the other to Divine Mother.

And how did my garden grow?

Employers were increasingly difficult. Child support stopped. Both boys were diagnosed with dyslexia, hyperactivity, and Attention Deficit Disorder at a time when very few people had heard of dyslexia, and ADD was something you didn't SUBRACT. Despite my support, Ty became shy from feeling different. He trudged to school every day with years ahead of him in which to confront a learning system neither he nor I could change, one so untailored to his needs no adult could have tolerated it. Linc's "I did it!" self-image cracked when the school's only solution for his ADD was a year of special education with children physically deformed and mentally retarded.

I didn't have the financial resources for outside help, so I taught myself about dyslexia; to inform those who did not know about it yet, I lectured on dyslexia; and to help dyslexic children, I created a non-profit foundation. Since they spent every day at school learning what they *could not* do, the foundation would provide opportunities to focus on what they *could* do; it would support all the creative, compensating gifts dyslexic children had been given genetically but had become too dispirited by low self-esteem to pursue. In this way, they could begin to feel good about themselves.

Ironically, the more good I did, the harder and darker things got; the ego was seeing to that, but I couldn't always see the ego, and I certainly couldn't see that darkness can inadvertently be a good sign: the closer we are to the light, the more darkness tries to keep us from it. I was too tired to see. My energy was suddenly in very short supply for someone only 36, and it was exacerbated by this:

Negative personality traits in my dear Alex, which had certainly taken their time being upfront about themselves, were now preventing a healthy realtionship. He had deliberately begun to keep me on the periphery of his life, he lied by omission, and he became increasingly arrogant, controlling, secretive, fearful, a separatist, a workaholic, a noncommunicator, and a keeper of the status quo devoutly unwilling to alter anything about his life to accommodate my needs.

In retrospect, these were classic characteristics of the ego. His had sprung up like mine as a defense against the light and love of Divine Mother; against the light and love between us, against his enlightenment and my part in it— and that meant he was falling into the same pattern as my mother, father and Michel, a pattern that denied me. Not realizing that I, too, was denying myself by avoiding Divine Mother, Alex's behavior was devastating. I didn't want to deal with it, but having Fanny's karma meant I couldn't leave him—I had done that once by dying.

There was another element at play in regard to Alex, one I was not aware of until he did a Divine Meditation with me years later: the animal symbolizing his inner nature at that time was an ostrich. What this meant in our lives is that he invariably avoided something as disquieting as change by shoving his head in the sand in the unconscious belief that if he did not appear to exist, the need for change would not seem to exist, either. The beautiful qualities of Henry were just as often submerged in the sand, forcing the negatives to become, like the feathers on the ostrich, *all* I saw.

Put that quivering ostrich with my deer ready to bolt and you have a couple who handled change about as well as if they had been locked in a zoo all their lives. And then factor in this: besides temerity, a fawn and deer symbolize harmlessness, a tender-heartedness and, like Bambi's mom, a vulnerabilty to the cruelty of men. As you have read, that was my karma; even the sexual abuse from my mother is typically associated with men. But I love men and that was putting me in an untenable position. As it turned out, however, being caught between a rock and a hard place was the best place; it would force the resolution of these matters. Even so, I didn't realize how important resolution was, and I certainly didn't realize that *almost every one of Alex's negatives applied equally to me.*

Our personality problems, common to many people, constituted an enormous blockade on the road to the unconditional love we all must have for one another. In our case, at least one of us had to change in order to snatch that zookeeper of an ego's key and make a break for freedom. But that seemed an overwhelming prospect at the time because only one of us was likely to try, and it wasn't Alex. Spiritual insight is one of the higher purposes of any relationship; we see the negatives in the other person so we *can* see them in ourselves and then change—but it was so much easier seeing them all in him.

And something had to be easy.

It was so hard to be responsible in the old ways now, so hard to fight back, so hard to keep my mind straight, so hard to carry on as I had before. But that was the point. However attached I was to them, the old ways of the ego *couldn't* work any more, not when new and enlightened ways had been introduced. The outmoded ego-thoughts, sitting in my mind like stubborn stains, would have to be bleached out by the light in what I now call "The Process of Spiritual Decontamination"—the removal of everything other than light. My life could then be rebuilt. That is what the baby in the bassinet at the cottage had symbolized all along: a new beginning, one wholly in the light of Divine Mother.

If I hadn't been busy building that dam to hide in or fleeing deeper into the forest, confusing my animal imagery because I was so confused, I might have poked out whichever head I had on at the time long enough to realize that—but I didn't. While so many of the interior experiences with Divine Mother had been uplifting, this step toward enlightenment required facing the ego; it required facing my own darkness.

Who wants to know that no mother, father, children's father or beloved from the annals of literary history had bequeathed any negativity to me, but had brought to the surface what was already *in* me? Who wants to know they were reflecting in magnified proportion *my own legacy to myself* from lifetimes without constant commitment to the light? And who wants to know not one of them could have tripped the trigger on low self-esteem if the gun hadn't been pointed at my own head at a point far earlier in time, when I was, at any time, capable of a far superior stance?

In truth, we all want to know because our freedom depends on it, but finding this out felt like being dumped into a compost heap at the back of the garden where each bit of refuse from my father, mother, Michel and Alex was not only theirs, but *mine*, too.

All I had to do was say, "Ok. I crēated this refuse myself," and ask Divine Mother how to dispose of it. That is all anyone has to do because any darkness made by the ego can be equally undone by the light. I just didn't see the pun on the word "refuse"—I had to refuse the darkness and stop refusing the light.

I don't remember Cinderella going through this with *her* Godmother, but then she probably didn't put up such a fight. After all, what's a bit of cinder and soot compared to a compost heap? But on the other hand—who really knows what happened between the bibbity-bobbity and the boo?

The next chapter explains what happened to me.

10

The Beginning of the End

In Divine Mother's Mind, filled with beautiful gardens, compost is a very valuable commodity. As any good gardener knows, the soil must be amended with decaying matter to help propel a seed out of the darkness of the earth into the light of day. It is the same for every soul. Divine Mother uses the refuse of our lives to help propel us out of the darkness of the ego into the light of God.

My reaction to this natural process was being unable to get out of bed, never mind the dirt. The reason for physical energy long on the wane but suddenly drained to that of an abandoned leaf-blower in 1985 was Epstein-Barre Virus, also known as Chronic Fatigue Syndrome, Adult Mononucleosis, and that illness back in boarding school which had unkindly revived itself when Ty was taken, Glandular Fever.

Chronic Fatigue can exist a few months or a lifetime. There is no cure to this day and, among its many possible causes, auto-immune deficiency topped the scale for me; there was no immunity from the psychological attack of the ego. The battleground had just shifted measurably from the false part of the mind to the entire body.

In the end, Divine Mother would prove to be all the immunity anyone *ever* needs, but, first, so you understand what She had to deal with, the Chronic Fatigue hit so hard so fast that the life force hovered near nil. Normal daily life became impossible, but the memory loss meant I couldn't always remember what that had been; the transition from health to illness had separated brain cells from thought like a laser. Friends vanished and I was left alone far too often with a host of allergies, spontaneous vomiting, headaches, anxiety, Candidiasis, aching pain in every limb, a low-grade fever, and raging unhappiness. Even my closest ally, a figure fitting a 5' 9" frame like a glove, stretched to 164 pounds of superfluous material and then shrank to 112 like a cheap cotton shirt. Adding insult to injury, my moods fluctuated as much as my weight; I couldn't control anything.

All the changes were so intense from the onset that I was a virtual invalid, a word constantly read by an increasingly demonic ego to mean that *I* was invalid, as in deficient, without value, not worth keeping. That view was only underscored when Alex almost completely disappeared, and I, without a brain, actually wondered in between trips to the bathroom to throw up ... *why doesn't he want to see me?*

The symptoms were not recognized world-wide as having a physical cause until 1986, so in my case only a few physicians working with a psychiatrist were willing to try a treatment other than bedrest, which was out of the question for someone with two hyperactive sons. But their severely limited knowledge led them to prescribe uppers (ritalin), downers (valium or ativan), anti-depressants (surmontil, nardil or xanax), and pain pills (tylenol with codeine)—all to be taken simultaneously in the bizarre belief that one would regulate the other; I wouldn't be too high or too low, but somewhere in between. It did work briefly, but when it didn't, the prescriptions weren't curtailed; the doctors just increased them to what I later, and almost posthumously, learned was the *highest* legal dosage.

"What is wrong with this picture?" Oh, yes. My mother took pills.

The negative side-effects of the "medicine" were so similar to the symptoms of Chronic Fatigue that it was impossible for the doctors, or me, to tell them apart. The slight difference between being sick and being drugged meant that no one realized over-medication had become a problem. In retrospect, the doctors were exceptionally unqualified to be experimenting chemically on me or others so desperately ill and so ill-advisedly drugged that we were not sufficiently in our right minds to refuse them. I had no insurance and little money, so I was more desperate than some; I had to work in order to support my children. The head of a hospital I met many years later emphatically pronounced the quality of this care as "Poor"—particularly since the illness was never correctly diagnosed as a spiritual crisis, the underlying cause of every disease.

With no immediate way out of the crisis, the illness or the drugs, I started drinking to numb the physical and emotional pain. "What is wrong with this picture?" Oh, yes. My mother drank.

Many months later, I confided my drinking to one of the doctors. Since his partner, the psychiatrist, kept an open beer bottle in his top desk drawer, this doctor's response to the very embarrassing confession of something I had managed to hide in shame from everyone was a jovial, "Well, if you don't like drinking, stop."

Had he informed me that the Candidiasis, a systemic yeast infection, literally craved the sugar in alcohol to grow; that the short half-life of the drugs meant they left my body daily and thereby initiated the *daily* withdrawal I met with alcohol; or that he knew of no way out of the overwhelming depression, the worst symptom of the virus, I never would have started. And had I been able to think clearly, I would have told him so instead of sitting there in engulfing shame because I knew by then I *couldn't* stop.

The depression persisted unabated with its characteristic emotional and mental contraction that diminished consciousness to the size of a Tic Tac. Since I was still astute enough to realize a breath mint wasn't a very good substitute for a mother, and that being utterly depleted hardly put me in a position to manage children who had enough energy to electrify an entire city during a blackout, there was no alternative but to send them to Michel. He had moved to Colorado by then, but I didn't consider the emotional cost of such a distance. Putting them on the plane was the hardest thing I ever had to do. After they left, I bought a canvas bag in the airport. On the front was printed, "Best Mom on Earth." It was true; Colorado would offer them advantages I couldn't contemplate giving then, and their absence would afford me the time and space to get well—wouldn't it?

The pain of their absence was so terrible, it felt every day as if someone had cut my heart out, and I got worse. These children had never been just my boys—they had been my buoys. Without them to keep me afloat, I couldn't even tread water and started to sink.

"What is wrong with this picture?"

Oh, yes. I had to live with my father when my mother was sick. But wasn't illness, drugs, alcohol, and depression some awful karma repeating itself unto the next generation ... and the next? When did it end?

Colorado was a new beginning for Ty; he didn't feel different there, but accepted instead. Linc, however, came back for two years. He had danced into the living room after returning for Easter vacation, *so* happy to be home. Aware there was little money because I couldn't work full-time, or often any time, he had whispered in his little seven-year-old voice, "Oh, please let me stay. I won't eat much."

That still makes me cry, and stay he did, providing enormous happiness, invaluable time together, and a way to hold on. But smarter than I, watching the alcohol and prescription drugs continue, Linc could see disaster in the offing when I couldn't yet envision such a dour end. He maintained what became a vigil by remembering, he said, a lifetime in which he'd had another mother like this. Linc knew what to do, but it was too much for anyone, let alone a child. He eventually decided on his own to go back to his dad and he was more than correct. I still admire his sagacity, but the vacuum he left behind filled with indescribable despair. Michel didn't have to resort to kidnapping for me to lose my children this time. I had done it to myself.

Negative emotions multiplied like bacteria growing in a petri dish and problems increased just as fast. There was financial help, just not enough to keep money from being a constant concern. The apartment was too expensive, but I would not move into a smaller one; without the second bedroom, the boys wouldn't have space of their own and, in my mind, might not come back. If I had the money to go to the market, the groceries stayed in the car; there was no energy to bring them upstairs, put them away and cook. Even so, there often wasn't the energy or desire to eat; nausea came with the illness, but I knew it had come too because I could not "stomach" what was going on.

Self-esteem, the dream class I had once gotten an "A" in, dropped from worthless to loathsome when the foundation for dyslexic children became too heavy to carry on my own and collapsed. A volatile relationship developed with Alex to the point of blaming and hating this once cherished person as surely as I was hating and blaming myself. Guilt rose to the surface and clung to me like grease to gravy for these situations and everything else in my life. I couldn't get out from under it, nor was there escape from the anger escalating over such an array of difficulties.

The dream on page 61, in which Divine Mother appeared for the first time and picked up one baby from the many bassinets in the room, began in a hotel complex. Our English word "hotel" derives from the Old French "hostel," functioning symbolically in the dream as a pun on the word "hostile"—and I was in such a complex form of hostility at this point that Divine Mother would have to lift me out of it just as She had lifted the baby from the bassinet.

The anger was further complicated by what began it, something that fluttered into my muddled mind as an evil event, but one I couldn't remember was sexual abuse. It *had* come up before, in a 1982 meditation and in shocking detail, when I was backtracking through time to find the last past life but came upon that incident instead. It was impossible for me to deal with—I later learned that the mother as perpetrator was not even addressed in therapy until 1985—and I didn't know to ask Divine Mother. I just forced it way back into the unconscious again where it was now bubbling up once more for the recognition that would ultimately result in my freedom from all of these negative conditions.

Sexual abuse was the first door to close on communiation with God, but not the last.

Once, working with Pia, I was taught psychometry, the reading of energy emanating from physical objects that gives information about the owner. A few days later, a new friend, Todd, whom I had met only briefly, visited with his friend I had never met, Mark. Deciding to try my new skills, Todd removed a ring for me to read. I held it in my hand and Divine Mother presented the image of a cloud over the sun, which I interpreted to mean that Todd was covering his own light. Mark then removed a lapel pin. I held it in my hand, but Divine Mother presented the same image: a cloud over the sun. I apologized, dismayed it hadn't worked, but both men laughed and admitted trying to trick me: the lapel pin really belonged to Todd and I had been right both times.

Well, by this point in the illness, I couldn't read the back of a cereal box, let alone an object, and I literally could not follow a sit-com, never mind Divine Mother, so another door on Divine communication had closed. And that was the terrible irony. Aiming only for the glorious goal of God by reconnecting with Divine Mother, I was ending up, all symptoms considered, a poster child for the ego.

"What is wrong with this picture?"

Oh, yes. Everything.

Far be it from me to know I was really a good witch without a cauldron, incapable of conjuring up even a sense of humor now. All I had by way of sorcery was a cat, and even that was there under duress since it had no way of escaping the third floor apartment. (I didn't open that door, either.) Still, there was *A Course in Miracles* saying the miracle I needed had nothing to do with magic: there was only one way to end this trial by fire and that was to reunite with the light forever. All the ego-hullobaloo would then be over, and to that end I became *A Course in Miracles* novitiate.

The book sat next to me on the couch when no one else would, nestled in my arms when it made sense and never seemed to mind being stuffed under a cushion when it didn't. As any reader can attest, its spiritual psychotherapy is difficult enough on a good day, but, I will add, next to impossible when you are sick, drugged, drinking and scared. Certainly these were serious obstacles to any goal of God, but illness, pills, intoxication and fear are invaluable instruments of the ego for exactly that reason; it's why so many of us are drawn to them.

Divinity was certainly within equal reach during this battle of good and evil wrought throughout the dark night of the soul. Christ would kindly present Himself in meditation—and out. As I learned first-hand, both He and Divine Mother can appear at will, but when you don't feel any more substantial than two sticky white calories, that is not always as comforting as it is unnerving.

This was especially true in the next step of spiritual decontamination: the advent of Christ Consciousness, an uncontrollable in-pouring and out-pouring of molten, golden light, doing its part to lift away the darkness. It was experienced without any awareness of its purpose or even that it had a name. But I did learn directly that this Christed light—the gift of Divine Mother through Her Son—does not depend on a meditative or altered state to manifest; it happens independently. It may include Christ's seen or unseen Presence, and often contains His Face as if in a kaleidoscope of light, forming and unforming, but always informing and transforming.

As often as that happened, I did not understand this *is* the Second Coming of Christ. The Second Coming pertains to each of us individually, *internally and in the mind,* because only the mind needs the healing that cures all ills: the unalterable restoration of truth and light to consciousness. When that authentically occurs, then we, too, have attained Christ Consciousness.

What I did know is that these manifestations of light were not hallucinations or fantasies. They occurred whether I was meditating, drinking, or medicating, and when alcohol and pills were sporadically banished from body and home. To believe otherwise, that Divine Mother cannot be effective in *any* state, is to try to limit the limitless. These experiences of the light were real, spontaneous, overpowering, and very frightening.

In retrospect, the terror was the ego's reaction to its own impending demise. The Christed light had come and only come after many prayers, including desperate novenas to St. Jude, following a change of heart from the illness: I still did not want to look at the ego, but I did want it gone. The light, then, was just going about its business of removing every underpinning of the ego *as requested.*

Thinking instead I had really gone around the bend, I bounced on and off the path in my own mind, undecided whether to follow God or the ego, even though my anxiety seemed to say the ego already had the upper hand and held me helpless in its grasp. After all, every negative belief ever emanating from that false mind, dislodged now by the light but not yet removed by it, was floating around me in nightmarish proportion without any indication of leaving.

Certainly the negatives were intensified by the drugs, alcohol and illness, but experiencing them so acutely created an indelible contrast to the calm, steady love of Christ and Divine Mother. At the time, however, it did not seem like a Divine Design to enable me to stop the ego in favor of God and therefore stop me from trying to serve two masters; it seemed like the end of the world.

Christ would kindly intervene in what was engulfing doubt about all my experiences in the light having led to utter calamity in my view by saying, "Oh, ye of little faith."

True enough, but when the efforts to re-align with God felt like free-falling into the abyss instead of rising to the top like cream, they hardly re-activated faith. Neither did the fact that every single time I went into Divine Meditation and met Christ, it was to see myself walking the wrong way on the path toward a real abyss. He would have to put His arm around me and turn me toward the light.

That was actually the good news; that is *why* He was there. But outside of meditation, the ego took over with a crushing rush of unanswerable questions:

"Why do you think spirituality works when it can't even make you walk the right way by yourself? And what aspirant to Divine Mother sends her children *away*? Come on! Who really talks to Christ? Who really sees the light of the Archangels? Who really meets God the minute She asks and then knows Him as *Her*? And why would you believe your grandfather's promise of a wonderful life when it's a disaster? Get a grip!"

I couldn't, not when I was alone, unable to be reached, unable to reach out, trapped in the amber of my own ambivalence and inabilities. Buried in this solitude, the ego was able to permeate my mind with its thinking to such an extent that I was made physically weaker by it. It depleted every internal resource in gruesome partnership with the Chronic Fatigue. And the more depleted I became, the more vulnerable, until the darkness had a new and unthinkable opportunity: it could and did pull in negativity from everyone around me, from the neighborhoods and cities surrounding me. I could *feel* it happening—I just couldn't find a way out now to save my life.

11

The Second Near-Death

A number of near-death survivors, particularly children who are still so close to heaven, acknowledge the presence of a beautiful, unidentified woman on the other side. Her light emanates peace and love, security and protection, guidance and good will. They have, of course, encountered Divine Mother. Many more recount the great light at the end of a tunnel. That, too, is Divine Mother.

I would certainly be with Her this next time around, but that would not be my immediate memory. Every near-death gives glimpses of the bigger picture for others to share, but it is designed to serve a need specific to the individual. In my case, it would present the opportunity to refuse the darkness.

Karma and destiny are symbolically represented by the number four. In June, 1989, four years after the Chronic Fatigue began, the anti-depressant Sinequan was prescribed to supplement the Prozac and other drugs. The combination was intended to reduce the depression, but it induced a rapid physical and psychological decline over the next six weeks. By the end of that time, the unholy trinity of drugs, ego and illness had reduced my mental focus to a blur and I couldn't see how to maintain the constant battle between faith and a lack of it. *With all my heart* now I wanted freedom from the ego and, despite the odds set up against it, the following graphically details how it happened. The symbolism of the events is so significant that the meaning is included in parentheses.

On August 12, 1989, I was drinking heavily to alleviate the depression which had become unbearable despite or due to the drugs. The potential suicidal side-effects of Prozac had not been made public then, so adding alcohol and Sinequan at least doubled the ante for disaster. Even though I wanted life, the ego had always wanted death and, with no strength left to fight it, I tried to slit my wrists.

There was the oddest polarity in my mind then, as if the ego had a very clear view of what was occurring, but the Divine had another, and I could simultaneously see both. Slitting my wrists seemed unstoppable from the ego's point of view, but I was equally aware of not really being a suicidal personality. If I were, I would have taken that way out, with more reason, a long time ago. So what was I *doing*?

I called Alex. Because I had used a serrated knife and only scraped up the skin, he laughed nervously and thought I was kidding, or so he later said. Instead of coming over, or calling 911 or even the police, he went to bed.

(Almost ten years later, I revisited the story of Fanny and read how Henry, like Alex, could not bear being near Fanny when she was dying. He, too, had retreated while it was happening.)

Sadly, I hung up the phone. It was then, through the Divine mind, that I noticed his mother's presence in the living room. It didn't concern me that she was dead and really should not have been there. Although I hadn't met either of Alex's parents before they died, both she and his father had vividly appeared before.

One night, years earlier, the smoke alarm in my bedroom had suddenly sounded for no reason. This was so unusual, like an alert, that I sat down on the bed and looked at it through the third eye. The face of a man appeared in gold light, superimposed over the alarm. He wore a pair of glasses that dissolved, reappeared and then dissolved again before he, too, faded away. I intuited this was Alex's father, which Alex later confirmed: his father had worn glasses in life, but didn't need them; they were an affectation. The manifestation and disappearance of the glasses, then, was his father's way of identifying himself to me in the light.

So I wasn't hallucinating or making up his mother's presence. It's just had I been in a better state, I would have realized what was going to happen—moms on the other side generally manifest outside of meditation to help us make the transition, too. My only thought, through the ego mind, was how nice it was of her to come when her son had not.

Not knowing what to do with myself (the false self), I went downstairs to empty the garbage (exactly what this night would do with the ego and its copious refuse). I found some large, discarded wooden shutters (symbolic of shutting out the light) in the dumpster (where shutting out the light belongs). I liked them (of course; shutting out the light while inviting it in was just what I had been doing the last few years, making myself sick in the process). I brought the shutters upstairs and put them on the floor in front of the television (symbol of the Divine telepathy running counterpoint to the ego). For some reason I went into the kitchen, maybe for another drink.

Returning to the living room, I had already forgotten the shutters were there, slipped on them (the slip in my life had been shutting out the light), and fell on my knees in front of the televsion (as if kneeling to the telepathic power of the Divine). I realized with extraordinary clarity and happiness that I was, at last, in the position of surrender which had otherwise been so difficult to make. It struck me as ironic. I had tried to surrender for so long and had managed it now by accident (there are no accidents). Somehow, by getting up, slipping, and falling again, backwards this time, I cracked my head on the wooden shutters (yes, I would have to be hit on the *head* to accept the light).

Not knowing it, I had sustained a deadly serious concussion. There was sudden, violent vomiting accompanied by the equally sudden, violent loss of sphincter muscle control (negativity would be emptied from me and released).

Very dazed, disoriented, and consumed with heat, I ripped off my clothes (stripping myself of one of the ego's nefarious allies, *attitudes*) and crawled naked over the beige carpeted floor on my hands and knees, vomiting from one end and defecating from the other. I crawled in circles from the living room to the dining room, into the cooler kitchen and back again, as if I could get away from the defecating and the vomiting and the heat, thinking, "What do I do? What do I do? I don't know what to *do*," (because only She knew), along with the ridiculous but quite astute concern, "I will never be able to get this out of the carpet."

I lost earthly consciousness then (lost the ego/negative mind) and "awoke" some time later with the realization that I had already left the body (illusion) behind.

Free of the body, and free of the drugs and alcohol in it, *an extraordinarily alert consciousness,* all that was left of me (the real me, the True Self), was already spiraling ahead into the darkness of death where I was not in a position to protest, resist, or disagree with anything. I remember saying to myself then as the deeply strange awareness of what was happening came with a name: "I'm—*dying*."

I recall, too, how strange it was to know unquestionably what was happening, when dying isn't experienced in advance. There is nothing on the earth plane or in Divine Meditation equal to that particular point in the transition.

Traveling at the speed of light through oblivion, the darkness encompassing me above and below, to the left and the right, well behind and definitely straight ahead, the realization came swiftly that I was going the wrong way. In fact, "Wrong Way"—written in gold-white light in the darkness and looking exactly like a freeway sign for wrong-way traffic—simultaneously materialized in front of me.

The choice had to be made *right then and there* to refuse the darkness and come back or in a second it would be

too late. With all the will I could muster, and there is an as-
tonishing amount at a time like that, I made the exceedingly
ultra-conscious decision to return.

Faith is Justified

I don't remember what happened immediately after
that or how the return was accomplished, but then this life-
altering event was not recalled for days, which certainly says
a lot about the severity of the concussion and the substantial amnesia following it. There was a large, painful lump on
the back right quadrant of my head, and on my right thigh
a bruise so purple it was almost black ... but no memory to
explain how these things had happened. I was engulfed with
shame to view the damage, thinking it the worst thing I had
ever done to myself; without the memory, I had no way of
knowing it was, as you will see, the best thing ever to happen to me.

When I did remember a few days later, it was very
sudden, out of the blue, and entailed a flood of information
and knowledge, as well as vividly *reliving* the near-death,
over and over, in the detail just given. Every time I shut my
eyes, I was instantly back in space, traveling at the speed of
light and experiencing the terrible awareness, "I'm dying."
It did not stop for five months. That is when I asked Divine
Mother to take it away on the promise that it would never
be forgotten, and She instantly reduced it to a memory.

I believe now that the recurrence was post-traumatic
stress, but the term was unknown to me then, as was what
the term near-death really meant. I did not realize that my
experience had that name until I happened to walk through
someone's kitchen a year later and heard a TV talk-show. I
came to a full stop, mesmerized by the details being given by
others who had experienced *so much of the same thing*.

The near-death, like so many aspects of my spiritual
life, was not externally confirmed until the experience had
been internally integrated. That was true even with the con-

cussion. My son Ty hit his head on the football field in Colorado during a game when I was there, also a year after the near-death. He was taken to the hospital for observation and released with the instructions to awaken him in the night to make sure he hadn't lost consciousness, and watch for memory loss, confusion, and vomiting. These were all symptoms of a severe concussion that could lead to death after a fall—and I had no idea until then that this part of my highly subjective experience had such an objective name.

Even though I fell on the night of the 12th, I did not come to until three days later, August 14, 1989, nine years to the *day* after lifting up my arms to God in my kitchen in Los Angeles following the first near-death. Nine is the spiritual number of completion and the near-death marked the end of a nine-year cycle of learning.

That end immediately brought a new beginning, the one represented by the baby in the bassinet at the cottage with Divine Mother. It was *radically* different from the past because all the learning prior to the near-death erupted during it into a freedom of Being that exists beyond what can be taught. In the blink of an eye, darkness turned to light, illusion to truth, suffering to joy, sickness to health, thinking to knowing, and my entire life to a sacred and holy form of communion with Divine Mother that continues to this day. I knew Her identity as irrevocable, consciousness continuing past the earth plane as self-evident, and doubt as impossible. Faith took up all the space left by the lack of it and my relationship with Divine Mother was restored to its purity in childhood, trust intact, the ego a dissolving memory.

Time was needed to absorb the enormity of what had actually happened, but I never wondered, "What is wrong with this picture?" It was all the truth and light.

Recovery in the Light

There are texts written at the time of Christ called the Gnostic Gospels in which the reality of Divine Mother is fully acknowledged. The Gnostic Gospels came to me as another after-the-fact confirmation; we will get to more of them later, but these selections are important just now:

1) The Gospel of Philip says, "Those who say they will die first and then rise are in error." Instead, they must "receive the resurrection while they live."

2) The resurrection, according to the *Treatise on Resurrection*, is "... the revealing of what truly exists [...] and a migration (a *metabote*, a transition, a metamorphosis) into newness."

These mean that whether the resurrection is enlightenment achieved during the graceful act of sitting in meditation under a Bodhi tree, or the rocket-booster propulsion of a near-death into the light, its effects—the revelation of what truly exists—must still be consciously recognized on the earth plane. In that way, illusions fabricated here can be recognized and refused *here*; the ego erected here can be recognized and dismantled *here*: "earth to earth, ashes to ashes, and dust to dust." Truth and light arise from the ashes in the aftermath of the *metabote* and we, like a steel phoenix, rise with them. When the truth and light are sustained *here*, the gates of heaven are permanently opened and we are free to leave the cycles of life on the earth plane.

The first action after my *metabote* into newness does not sound nearly so high-falutin.' You have to start where the booster-rocket drops you, and I did, migrating at a crawl across the kitchen floor through all those ashes the day I came to after the near-death. I picked up the telephone and, with a flap of little phoenix wings, called AA: "Help me."

I promptly passed out again and didn't know the call had been made until I found the phone book open to the "A's," and angels from AA came that evening to take me to a meeting. Of that, I recall a car door handle; wobbling in and out of consciousness in a room stifling hot even for August, and being looked at in alarm because my physical condition was so very poor. Compare this in-the-body state to the ultra-conscious invincibility without a body only hours before, and it's no wonder getting those wings to flap like a phoenix right off the bat was a bit hard.

In order to fly at all, Divine Mother counseled me to do the next day what I later learned is never advised, at least not without your Godmother close by: go cold turkey off the drugs and alcohol. Now that could not have been a pretty sight, lying on the couch, shivering and shaking, muscles involuntarily spasming, feet uncontrollably splayed, but I wasn't alone anymore, and, when She said, "It's all right. It's like a roller coaster ride at Magic Mountain with your children, it *will* end," I believed Her.

The withdrawal did stop some days later, and it included something that didn't seem humanly possible: I was awake 52 hours straight before sleeping naturally, but only for an hour, until my body began to regulate to life without the drugs. And then—there was a knock at the door.

This announced one of the first of many obviously Divine communications arriving in human and almost comical form, the messages were so clear. When I answered the door, it was to find two cable men, whom I had not called, standing on the threshold. They had mysteriously arrived to check the connections. One of them went up on the roof to fiddle with something, while the other poked at my VCR near the front door. After a moment's pause, the one inside yelled up to his co-worker on the roof, "SHE'S ALIVE!"

Oh, thank God. I needed to hear that because, who could tell? Everything was suddenly so different when only my mind had changed. I could see truth now—and *nothing* was ever seen the same again.

First, I was connected, all right, and without meditation to achieve it. My eyes literally opened wider and wider, eagerly surveying in mirrors the unmistakable and amazing sight of a *joyous* woman, alight with laughter and good cheer, smiling back at me. It was Joy, the True Self that Divine Mother had shown me in the mirrors of that great room during the Divine Meditation detailed in Chapter 1. I was, at last, Joy.

I could see, too, that everything leading to the near-death had not occurred to undo me as I had felt, but to undo the ego in favor of God. In the process, this related promise from Christ in *A Course in Miracles* was fulfilled: the conscious shift from fear to truth.

The conscious shift from fear to truth is the conscious shift from the ego to God, from darkness to light, from ignorance to knowing, from illusion to Reality. For me, it had literally happened in an instant, just as *A Course in Miracles* says it will, and it happened because the oblivion I entered during the near-death and consciously refused was the abyss of fear we each must cross over to reach the other side. Whether it is the other side of a physical death (into spirit), the other side of the ego (into God), the other side of darkness (into light), the other side of ignorance (into knowing) or the other side of illusion (into Reality), that is what crossing over means. We return the way we came, and the way we came to anything contrary to an absolute state of Being, the way we came even to this planet as you will see in a subsequent chapter, was through and due to the fear of our own making.

The fear of death is the parent fear we all entertain; it spawns every other fear. But the near-death proved to me *by direct experience*, and experience was the key, that *consciousness is what we are and consciousness continues. There is no death.* This knowledge enabled me to refuse the darkness of oblivion and the fear it represented as the Wrong Way so categorically that fear has never returned.

Once this purpose of the near-death was served, I did not immediately need the conscious memory of continuing into the light. I knew the light. She had been with me since I was a little girl. What I didn't know is that darkness is not evil or fearful. It is, in fact, as neutral as everything else that exists. We just project our fears onto the darkness and, in so doing, give darkness extraordinary negative clout.

How I was empowered to refuse the darkness, however, was due to something else. Remember the many times

Christ appeared in meditation to turn me around on the path when I was going the *wrong way*? I didn't know it then, but His guidance had been a true dress-rehearsal for the near-death. Because of so many practice sessions with Him, I knew exactly what decision to make at the critical moment, when I wouldn't otherwise have known.

That knowledge is never lost, so it has been possible since the near-death to be telepathically aware of friends and others who, in spirit, have arrived in my living room for help getting to the other side when they "die." I enter a meditative state and, at their telepathic request, help them cross over. This can be a very apprehensive period for them if fear still exists; the abyss appears enormous, when it is just an illusion created by fear. After offering calm and comforting words of faith and love, I take their hands in mine, maintain strict eye contact, and we walk together over the abyss as if gliding on glass. In that way we "cross over" to the Woman ready to receive them at the entrance to light and a cornucopia of worlds of light beyond: Divine Mother.

Assisting in this way is akin to Christ helping Peter walk on water for this reason: water is a metaphysical symbol for illusion. As long as there was no illusion of fear to obstruct him, Peter could walk on water. Once fear entered in, however, he sank into the sea, and Christ said, as He had so often said to me, "Oh, ye of little faith."

True faith is knowing. Knowing is without illusion, and it was by knowing that Christ proved it is possible to overcome the world's perception of fear. That is what it means to overcome the world. That is what it means in our own lives when we make the conscious shift from fear to truth. That is what it means to end the need for further lives on this particular plane.

Another reason to conquer fear is that every illness is fear-based; when fear is removed, there is no illness. The most concrete example of this, and of the fundamental change in my life, was immediate health. I literally danced down the street only two days after the near-death, singing

Gershwin's, "I'll build a stairway to Paradise with a new step every day. I'm going to get there at any price, step aside, I'm on my way!"

Recovery in the light didn't make me Ginger Rogers, but it certainly made me happy. And there is no mystery why this song from "An American in Paris" came to mind. The light of God I had tried to give to my father in Paris had been abundantly returned to me.

The near-death did something else concerning him. The removal of the ego had shifted intellectual thinking, to which I had so objected in my father and was unable to transcend by myself, into the direct knowing of God that had been my experience as a child in the garden. As a result, and after years of an academic parroting of *A Course in Miracles* at best, I could open it at random right after the near-death and *know* what it meant. This was such a delight, like finding Santa has come in the night, that I kept doing it, line after line, "I understand this!"

The transition from thinking to knowing is possible because *without the ego, there is nothing but the light of knowledge.* That is the light of truth, the light of Divine Mother, and our birthright as Her children.

All of this and more can be achieved *without* a near-death by following in upcoming chapters the specific ways Divine Mother has devised for it. I had to experience the ways myself, as you will see, but I knew as soon as they happened that they are valid and true:

Going over them on the other side was what I hadn't been able to recall about the near-death.

12

Knowing

When you are no longer who you thought you were,
but who you really are, it takes time to adjust. For
over a year and a half, a mother again in Colorado with my
children, I felt like my own walk-in. It was as if another soul
had come to take my place, because I had *such* a different
mind:

I knew now from direct experience what Grandpa had
reached out to teach me about life and life-after-death; what
my children had always known and never had to learn; how
to use free will wisely by listening to Divine Mother, and
how to see in the present and live in the moment, because
the ego and the past, wiped out, weren't in it. There existed
only a weightless mind in a profoundly expanded state of
Being with more than enough room for Divine Communication to flow naturally through. Without teaching, all was
learned, just as without asking, all was given.

The Importance of Truth

Part of the knowing that came without learning was
to tell the truth. Despite seeking the truth for so long, there
had seemed so many reasons to lie, from the advent of the

ego straight through to the near-death.

My mother's mental illness was a taboo subject in the suburbia of the 1960's and literally could not be discussed. A counselor at Arcadia High School finally retrieved information from me about her real condition when I ran out of excuses for missing class to care for her. My mother was sent to a mental institution the next day and I was sent to Paris the next month, so telling the truth was hardly safe. Across the ocean, my father forbade criticism, but not being able to say what I thought only hid the truth from me. Since he denied emotional truth as well, I learned to conceal my feelings, but that also hid them from me. I kept the Golden Girl from him and everyone else in order to protect her, but that too kept this source of beauty and strength from me.

Back in America, I was not honest about the status of my relationship with Michel or the quirks of his personality, but that deluded me. Alex's ego had so compartmentalized his life in order to control it that I came to find myself in one of its tiny pockets. Instead of declaring my needs equal to his, I let the self-erasure developed from my ego subjugate them to his self-interest the way women used to do, and I pretended to be happy to please him. Denial did not work any better for this woman than had for any other: it allowed him to believe his attitude was acceptable and correct; and that meant, in his mind, that my being "irrational" and angry in reaction to it was unacceptable and wrong, diminishing me further. Chauvinism may have been all right in the 19th century when we last knew each other, but it wasn't all right in this one, and alcohol became the ego's tonic for the pain of self-denial, the torturous consequence of not insisting on the truth.

For whatever reason, there had been no safe place in my life to express the truth. Therapy was unequal to the task of understanding spirituality, reincarnation and karma, the healing factors inherent in every problem or concern, so it was not a good route for me.

Once, for example, after Michel had taken Ty, I went

to a therapist named Betty. I arrived for one appointment with two photographs placed back to back; one was a head shot of me, the other of Mary taken from Michelangelo's *Pieta*. I was still stumbling with my spirituality then, seeking Divine Mother without knowing it and having only Mary as a representation. I was also trying to meld who I am as a human being with who I am as a divine being, which was obvious from the placement of the photographs; there are two parts to me, as there are two parts to each one of us. Instead of understanding this, the woman viewed me as if I should be standing outside a Greyhound bus station somewhere and I never went back—but her reaction only kept my divinity from me, and it kept it from me for a long time. Then, even when I firmly found Divine Mother again, society was unready to accept Her. As a consequence, there was so little support for what I knew to be true that I wasn't free to talk about Her—but that only kept Divine Mother from me.

Any denial, then, no matter how it came about, only hurt *me*—as it only hurts each one of us. The emotional deceit accompanying it ultimately placed me where the work on symbolism would not let it be missed: in a "lying" position, flat on my back with Chronic Fatigue, and then flat on my back just about dead. I *had* to tell the truth after the near-death to survive, as we all do, and I did.

This was particularly difficult with Alex for the reasons noted, but also because of his intense resistance to metaphysics and Divine Mother; he could go deaf at the mention of either one. But leave it to Divine Mother to put the one person who really didn't want to hear it with the one person who really had to say it. The friction from that alone would create the heat to cook up something really great, or make us get out of the kitchen altogether. As it turned out, and on Her advice that I "Override his objections to truth. *He must hear you*," I started talking no matter what the reaction—and he hasn't stopped listening since.

Even small white social lies and omissions are unacceptable because they are so dangerous. Not only are we de-

ceiving others, we are deceiving ourselves. The internal message, rarely conscious but extremely impacting, is that *we are
not trustworthy*. Deeply betrayed by our own lack of integrity, we stop trusting ourselves—and the dust from that
alone becomes the dirt that becomes the grime that keeps
the light from us, and us from the light. It is that simple and
that catastrophic.

The soul cannot tolerate lying for another reason: the
personality splinters into interior pieces, one for each lie or
omission. It only seems to us that no harm is done, but the
damage actually occurs in the unseen disintegration of the
keeper of those lies, the mind; and then in the disintegration
of the keeper of the mind, the body. The causal relationship
between body and mind was so obvious to me that, once
whole again and *integrated* from the near-death, there was no
question that the continued health of both body and mind
required and got my *total integrity*.

A Course in Miracles says as early as Chapter 1, "When
you have become willing to hide nothing, you will not only
be willing to enter into communion but will also understand
peace and joy." This is so true and vitally important that it
can't be emphasized enough. I've even written it on a piece
of paper like a fortune cookie and popped it into the pockets
of people I know, just to keep the message available to them.

Other truths that came in without learning involved
the importance of words. Karma, for example, is created by
our thoughts, *words*, and deeds. How many times have we
heard people say, "Oh, I could just kill you," "I'm so stupid!"
or "I have the monster this week-end." We say things that
we absolutely do not mean and don't consciously hear. Not
only do these words enter the unconscious mind of the person being spoken to, and our own as well, but *all* words are
creators. Many times before the Chronic Fatigue, I had said
about certain conditions, "This is making me sick," and sure
enough, they did.

There are also great truths in words hidden from view
by a single letter. For example, the word "altar" is only one

letter away from the word "alter," yet on reflection they are synonomous. If our life condition needs to be altered, we need to go to the inner altar for transformation and change. The shift from "holy days" to "holidays" certainly put a new spin on December every year, just as the remarkable transition from "plane" to "planet" has led us to believe that intelligence other than our own comes from different planets without regard to the reality of intelligence coming from different planes of existence.

The true meaning of particular words was received after the near-death, too. For instance, the word "respect" really means "to look again"—at ourselves, at others and at God to see the light within. Respect in this sense breeds respect as we otherwise know the word; by "looking again" we can find ways to honor the light in everyone. Sustained consciousness in the light depends on respect, on kindness and on simple politeness. In fact, being respectful, kind and polite came in very strongly as the *only* way to Be.

The real meaning of "obey," as in "love, honor and obey," was given as well. Obey does not mean submission to another's will. It derives from the French and means to hear, or, as it was elucidated to me, *to hear the other person and answer them*, making the vow a pledge of compassion and understanding that serves a marriage and all of our relationships. The meaning of "independence" came, too. It never means separation from God, but being *in*-a-state-of-*dependence* on God. When we look to Her for answers and solutions, we not only receive them, we are made free by them.

The more this was realized, the more I went to Her. The result has proven what did not seem possible before. I am never led astray, and every moment includes Her as an active participant in my mind. Constant communion exists because the imagined barriers between the two minds was dissolved when recognition of our eternal oneness with God was restored by the near-death. And in the constant, conscious communion resides unparalled security in the endless love, light and truth all around.

When Karma Ends

Answers to my question, "When does karma end?" raised during the episodes which so mimicked my mother when I was ill, were also made known. Negative karma begins the moment we disengage ourselves from the awareness of our oneness with God and tolerate the psychological separation. By the same token, negative karma begins to disintegrate and then end when we consciously realign with God. Like the ego which manufactured it, negative karma cannot withstand the light of Divine Mother.

Any situation or ailment from which we suffer is the karmic result of stepping away from the light in that area. Retracing our steps back into the light with Divine Mother cancels the karma. We will go into much more of this later, but as an example just now, Fanny Appleton died at 43. The near-death, a victory instead of a tragedy, occurred for me at the age of 41. The karma of an early death, which could have become mine again, did not happen. It was overcome by Divine Mother who is in charge of life *and* death.

The Unknowable

This next story is quite an abrupt departure, but it is nonetheless part of the knowing that came without learning. Kitty and Jose Menendez were murdered in Beverly Hills a few days after the near-death. I knew exactly who did it, and it was not the Mafia publicly presumed at the time. Seven months later, my mother called me in Colorado and said, "You'll never guess who they just arrested in those Beverly Hills murders."

"The sons."

"How did you know! It was just reported this second."

I shrugged, "I always knew."

Better I had known something more useful, perhaps, like how to create Divine Mother Software to talk with Her at the push of a button, but there it is. The idea that became the Larry Sanders Show was given, too, a couple of times. Maybe at that moment it was being put to paper for the first time or the deal was being signed; it doesn't matter. What matters is that, as with the Menendez brothers, I was in an ultra-receptive state after the near-death. An open mind has been maintained over time by ignoring what the world says and listening only to Divine Mother. Anyone who does this consistently becomes receptive to virtually every truth in the air. The following story is noted here as a very concrete example.

Having returned to California from Colorado, I was writing at home one evening and suddenly knew my son Ty, by then 18, was in terrible danger in Colorado. Since he was out that night and could not be reached, I immediately got on my knees and prayed for his safety and protection.

Ty called the next day. An hour or so after the prayer, he had been driving on an ice-slick road and swerved to avoid a bus coming from the opposite direction. His car slid around backwards and fish-tailed off a very steep embankment, turning over three times in a frozen field until it came to a stop upside down. Ty, too, was upside down, hanging mid-air inside the car, saved from serious injury and death by his seat belt.

"Mom," he said, "I never wear a seat belt. Something just told me to put it on right before the accident and I did." That "something" was the answer to a mother's prayer.

Clairvoyance like this is our natural state, and it is because only one Consciousness exists: the Conscious Mind of God in which the individual attributes of the Mother and Father converge. It encompasses each one of us and literally resides *in* each one of us, just like the double helix of a single strand of DNA resides in each cell of the body.

Everything is known to this Mind. Since we all share in it by being part of it—and since we are all linked to one another through it, just like catenated cells in the body—everything is known to us, too. There are no mysteries, not even about the universe; it only seems that way because we have habitually closed our minds to what is really in them.

Now one bit of very pressing knowledge coming in a day or two after the near-death was decidedly odd because it came without explanation: an obligation to be a stand-up comedienne. This had never been a desire and there was no way I could see it happening. After all, who would want to listen to someone battered and bruised after knocking herself out cold with some *shutters*?

But ways opened up. One is the classes, lectures and Guided Divine Meditations I give now for others to meet Divine Mother, and another is this book, because what the obligation meant was "Stand up," (a good start, since I'd been flat on my back for years), "tell the truth," (fine, since I finally knew what it was), "and be funny about it, for heaven's sake," because recovery in the light really means being able to see the humor in everything.

A Course in Miracles says one reason the ego exists is that we forgot to laugh and by the omission forgot we are inviolate and protected. That invulnerability and safety can be seen as incontrovertible fact in the aftermath of the near-death. Nothing negative in my life had ever had an effect on me, not on the *real* me. Just like the waves on the shore when I was 15 years old, there was no effect on the innate integrity of the soul. That is the truth or I never could have survived and found the Self untouched, knowledge intact, my own light shining. There is nothing, not even death, that can destroy our Being. We only think it can.

Conscious Participation

As noted at the end of the last chapter, specific ways to become one with the light and receive direct knowledge without the headache of a near-death had actually been part of my near-death. I could use those ways in my own life and verify their importance through demonstrable, personal experience for others to use in their spiritual pursuits.

One way which came into my life only ten days after

the near-death was balancing our Western philosophy with Buddhism and chanting from the East. In conjunction with Divine Mother, each one would substantially help me understand the *origin* of any remaining issues, and articulate the means by which negative karma can be dissolved.

According to Divine Mother, the fastest way to enlightenment is to follow "The Spiritual Process," something extensively detailed in an upcoming chapter with that title. But a significant element of the process to share just now is our *conscious participation* with the light to resolve situations, problems and concerns—which is to say, pray as we will, God doesn't do it all. The negativity we have made here, don't forget, we can and are actually required to unmake here. There is little point to having Divine intervention in a situation if we don't know how we created it. If it is solved for us, without our being privy to the mechanics of the solution or at least privy to how and when the mistake was made, we will be free only as long as it takes to make the same mistake again. If, on the other hand, we know how we created a negative situation or got into one, we will be too alert and aware to do it again. This is particularly true if the knowledge is made available to us from *direct experience*, not mental analysis, deduction, theory, or just being told.

The easiest way to understand how something negative began is to participate consciously with Divine Mother in a direct experience of the inherent cause of the problem or concern, and its solution. The following is an excellent example of exactly what that means.

Divine Mother's wand of light had been very effective on this Cinderella, but there was still an adjustment to make on one of the undergarments, on the "slip" as it were, beneath my new ball gown: the "slip" into anger. The conscious participation required to *begin* removing it occurred in May, 1990, six months into life in Colorado when there was a mix-up at the school regarding my son Linc. I became angry out of all proportion, openly so, which hadn't been my style. Minimizing and hiding the anger had been.

As I chanted long and hard to resolve the anger, having a drink after nearly a year of sobriety not only became a good idea, but an important one. There was a lesson in it that had to be experienced with these new eyes. I don't recommend anyone doing this without their God Mother consciously at hand, *but on the strength of Her verification that something otherwise wrong would prove right,* I had the drink. Looking at the glass in my hand, the lesson came as clear as a bell: anger, another aspect of the ego, had turned in on me as depression and illness, both of which had turned in on me as alcohol and prescription drugs—almost turning me into a corpse. In all of its various forms, my anger at other people had never done anything but ricochet back to hurt *me.*

A variation on an old rule came immediately to mind: "What I think I do to you, I actually do to myself."

I will, therefore, value you as I value myself and do unto you as I would have you do unto me, because that is exactly what happens. What I do to you *is* done to me, if not by you, then by another; and if not in this lifetime, then in another. That is law of karma, the law of cause and effect, the law of direct experience.

The purpose of karma, however, is far from malicious. What we send out is sent back in order to let us know that there *is* only one Mind here: what affects you *does* affect me. No thought, word or deed—past, present or future—is without this mirrored consequence. What we send out is returned to us because we only judge what we do not understand. But experiencing karma first-hand actually *creates* understanding. We know from experiencing it ourselves exactly how, and why, another person feels or behaves as they do in the same situation.

The beauty of this is that when karma occurs, a domino effect always ensues: once there is understanding, there is no judgement against ourselves or another; once there is no judgement, there is compassion; once there is compassion, there is no personal attack or hurt; once there is no attack or hurt, there is no anger; once there is no anger, there is only freedom. The end result of freedom makes kar-ma *our personally created and directly experienced <u>salvation</u>*.

Because all of this was so clearly understood by direct experience, I haven't had a drink since that time and I have never been angry again. Rather, I adhered to two lines from *A Course in Miracles*:

1) "Anger is never justified."

2) "If something causes you upset, there is another way of looking at it."

It actually got to be fun because if anger even said hello, I said goodby and went off to Divine Mother to find "another way." She always told me what it was, and *why*, providing key information which had otherwise been lacking in the situation. What She said made it entirely understandable, forgiveable and/or pointed toward new action on my part. Instead of being something negative, then, anger was transformed into an adventure in happiness because the outcome was always joyous. Eventually the anger stopped presenting itself as a possible reaction, something that was verified not only by my own emotions, but by a dream:

A rough and tumble sea went underground from the beach, beneath some very steep cliffs and then deep into the earth, ending below a great mountain. I was standing on top of the mountain, very happy.

In the morning, working on the symbolism, I knew the sea was emotion, and a stormy one meant anger. It followed a certain path that was hidden from view and I was standing over it at a point where I could clearly see it ended. Thinking aloud, I said, "Ok. I'm standing over it. I'm over it—oh, I'm over it!" I had gotten over my tendency to anger.

Now, conscious participation certainly does not always require a step back into darkness to see the light as it did with the drinking. For instance, after returning to California in 1991, my son Linc came to live with me. Divine Mother had predicted this two years earlier when it seemed impossible he would ever leave his friends in Colorado. What She did not say, however, is that this would entail putting my "adventure in happiness" to the ultimate test: living with a 16-year-old.

But this was not any 16-year-old. Linc had just been told by his father, "I never wanted you. You were your mother's idea."

Forget for the moment it took two to make this child, because Michel did, even days later when I confronted him over the telephone about the devastating effect that comment had on our son. His reply was, "I meant it. I feel fine about it." Ok, so forget Michel for the moment, and let's look at the one who really mattered here: Linc. His erratic personality at the time was due in part to the needless pain of this unretracted statement, but it was also due to his being a teen in general: angry, hormonal, ego-driven. Since I had been at his birth, I knew the poor child wasn't himself and, for all the reasons just given, I knew why.

Since Divine Mother had been at my birth, and knew why I wasn't myself during my adolescent tantrums as an adult, I decided to take after Her example: as She had held in Her Mind the image of who I really am, I would hold the image of Linc and not crack under his tantrums, either. I refused to validate any variance with that image by reacting to it and would only respond by saying, "Linc, the truth is, you are a better person than this. When will you see it, too?"

Well, bless his heart, Linc didn't understand this approach, not when he more than anyone could provoke me to anger. He kept upping the ante until one night he finally threw his arms around me in the car, exhausted from every trick in the book to break me, and literally in tears, cried in desperation, "Mom, I'm being so bad—you *have* to react!"

My voice was so calm and assured I almost thought it was Divine Mother's. "No, I don't, Linc. You have to stop trying to make me react, because look at what it's doing to *you*."

He did. I watched as he picked up his head and surveyed himself wedged between me and the steering wheel, tears streaming down his face. I saw him realize then that the only person any of his behavior had hurt was the one crying in the car with his arms around me. From that time on, Linc has worked to dismantle the ego in favor of the precious being of light who came to me at his birth.

Now, back in Colorado and back in time for just a bit, moving out of anger that night with a drink had another very important benefit. It had paved the way for my resistance to Linc's angry ego at 16, and it also required my conscious participation.

Enormous sadness, previously submerged by alcohol and anger, could finally surface in what I call "The August of Great Grief." I spent those weeks coinciding with the one-year anniversary of the near-death experience in front of my altar, doubled over, insuppressibly sobbing, "I'm so sorry, I'm so sorry, I am so, so sorry,"—for listening to the ego; for putting myself through so much pain instead of accepting truth and light when it was presented; for suffering at the hands of my family which, without an accurate perspective, was part of the pain I not only felt but gave to others; and for letting my Golden Girl down by not reuniting with Divine Mother sooner.

Unspecified grief came up, too, waves of sorrow followed by uncontrollable apology that such a stubborn will had deprived me and others of happiness and joy over any lifetime, remembered or unremembered. Errors from them all, not detailed but nonetheless emotionally profound, rose up as if they were happening right then, all at the same time, riding on the waves of grief for the only recognition that would bring release: mine.

This kind of experience is most often met on the other side when, with the die cast so to speak, we are shown the effects of our negativity on others and on ourselves with little opportunity apart from another lifetime to rectify the injustice. I didn't have to be shown. Once the grief surfaced, I knew—*but it did have to be felt.* The karma could not stop until the underlying pain and sadness personally caused had been personally experienced and recognized, or, as the word "recognized" literally means, "known again."

As you will see, concrete details about specific karma would later be given, but when just this much was done, my voice had permanently dropped an octave and laughter was loosened from my throat, when both had been at an almost strangulated pitch all my adult life. These were very significant markers of emotional freedom, as was the realization that by way of apology I had finally taken responsibility for *all* the circumstances in my life.

As a result, I was able to turn my attention next to the one person anger had kept me from dealing with until this point: Alex. What happened, quite apart from telling him the truth, is included here because it beats so deeply at the heart of every relationship.

I understood directly from Divine Mother, and from the knowing that came in the aftermath of the near-death, that the relationship with Alex had to be recovered in the light and cherished by us both. This was clearly part of our combined mission, particularly since I'd already died young as Fanny, leaving him to spend the remaining *decades* of his life as Henry alone. I had ducked out of a lot of unfinished business then and would not be allowed to do it again, for both our sakes.

There was an additional reminder to make the effort, too—one I stared at every day out my window in Colorado. "The Rockies may crumble, Gibraltar may tumble, they're only made of clay, but ... our love is here to stay." That was just a fact to be reckoned with. While much of my old life had been left behind and good riddance, Alex could not be dismissed as part of the past.

But my feelings about him then were very conflicted. By the end of the illness, he had all but vanished and virtually abandoned me the night of the near-death. He had let me "die" ...

... but with eyes that could see, and with other emotions at ease, it was impossible not to notice now the greater truth. His absence had allowed me to Live.

A Course in Miracles says everyone will play their part in our awakening. It hadn't occurred to me that absentia could or would be a part played by anyone, but it is; Alex did it. So how to assess his absence? If I decided he had let me "die," that would mean judging him wrong, when judging him at all would create the anger capable of hurting *me*. If I chose understanding instead, by realizing that his not being there did not matter as much as the fact that it had let me live, then we *both* would be free—free to love ourselves, each other, and everyone else with a selflessness that had not existed before.

Thanks entirely to Divine Mother's direct guidance and encouragement, and Her insistence on my authentically coming to it, understanding was chosen and true selflessness became the reality. That choice altered me in ways that have profoundly altered Alex. By way of a small but very significant example, the animal which now symbolizes his nature is not the ostrich; it is the same as mine—a tender-hearted, harmless deer.

Choosing to understand also provided this cherished overview: had I not been given the opportunity of the near-death experience, I would not have fully embraced Divine Mother. Without Her, I would not have realized my true identity as Her child, re-established the joy of Being, found the freedom to love, or, as you will read in the next chapter, known enlightenment in direct relationship with Her.

Everyone has benefited from what happened to me. Even when they were unaware of the means of change, the effect rubbed off in kind. This was so clearly shown by Linc when he, at the age of 18, cashed a hard-earned paycheck and went to Magic Mountain for the day with a friend. Expecting a call in the evening about his wonderful day, I heard instead of even hello, "Mom! I'm so sorry. Oh, I'm so sorry."

I gulped. He had wrecked the car, knocked his friend off a roller coaster, punched out Daffy Duck. "Oh, honey—what happened?"

"I didn't know how much Magic Mountain cost. All

those times I made you take me when I was little. I didn't know. I'm so sorry. I am so, so sorry."

When there is no anger, there is plenty of room for apology, compassion, and love all around.

13

Around the World

How could the fundamental Reality of Divine Mother, which had altered every aspect of my life, not be common knowledge?

That question began the earnest search for evidence of Divine Mother outside my own experience late one night, not long after the near-death. There was a snowstorm in the Colorado Rocky Mountains. I was lying upstairs in bed, listening to the wind brush snow across the roof and wrestling with that very disturbing question.

In the East

Hard to imagine the answer came while nestling under a comforter instead of scouring a library or seeking out sages, but that is exactly what happened. The *Lotus Sutra,* a highly revered teaching of the Buddha, telepathically came to mind as Divine Mother's response to my question. These quiet cues from Her are always to be followed, no matter how unrelated they may seem, and that is what I did: Sutra means a "teaching" ... and the lotus ...?

The light went on. One of Divine Mother's symbols is a white or gold rose, but another symbol, irrelevant before without a knowledge of Buddhism, is a white or gold *lotus*.

A moment passed before another light came on. The *Lotus Sutra* is described by Buddhists as "the lantern in the darkness." Divine Mother had come to me in the very first meditation carrying a lantern in the darkness, nine years before Buddhism was even a thought in my head.

I nearly fell out of bed because these two pieces combined meant, to me, that the *Lotus Sutra* had been received by the Buddha *from Her*.

There was further reason to think so. The opening of the sutra states that the Buddha "serenely arose from meditation" and spoke spontaneously, saying, "There is no ebb and flow of birth and death, nor life in this world and later extinction." How did He have this uncompromising knowledge of eternal life? Buddhists say it came from His own enlightenment, and I agree, *but what does that mean*? To me, it meant that his enlightenment had come directly from the *Source of enlightenment*, from the Source of all light and truth in or out of meditation: Divine Mother. But I had no proof of this, at least not then in 1990.

On *Mother's* Day of 1993, however, and living in Los Angeles, there was an inner directive from Divine Mother to drive to Ojai, about an hour away. I had never been there before and only vaguely recollected that the Indian teacher and philosopher, Krishnamurti, may have lived there at one time. I didn't ask why this request was being made; sometimes a mystery is better experienced than it is explained.

The Ojai Valley was more breath-taking than Aspen Valley. Instead of white snow against a mountain backdrop, groves of white-blossoming orange trees grew against a purple-blue mountain border. The presence of heaven sparkled the light, purified the air, scented the flowers and made the mountains embraceably close, culminating in a sense of the sacred I had not experienced in a physical location since being in the garden as a little girl.

Directed then to walk through the groves in the crystal clear sunlight, I noticed on every tree an array of pink tight buds, open white blossoms, some fruit as small as tiny green nuggets, others large and ripened, a few wizened and shrunken in decay. All the various stages of development were present; the entire process of fruition was occurring simultaneously on a single tree. I thought this was just like us. We are in constant developmental motion from birth to old age; some emotional, mental or psychological aspects mature while others begin to bud, and still others wither and die. But Divine Mother intervened in my thinking, asking me to look again—at the bigger picture this time.

Stepping back, I did. All the stages of the life-cycle occurring at one time was a vivid illustration of simultaneous cause and effect. If we are like this orange tree spiritually, and that was Her point, then what are the stages of our lives simultaneously producing in us? What are they really for? The answer rose right up: *clarity*. Each stage ultimately produces clarity, making the real fruit of any life the capacity to *see*, to see Reality and see it as I could not help seeing it at that moment—with the assistance of profoundly clear light all around.

Our physical, mental, emotional and psychological maturation follows pre-determined developmental stages, each one holding the potential for the next. But there is no potential in Reality. It is already there. This means that in the same way the reality of the orange tree is already there, whole and complete despite all the simultaneous stages going on within it, the Reality of *who we are* is already there— whole and complete despite the simultaneous changes going on within us.

Because Reality is whole and complete, it does not require development. In other words, we do not need to develop wisdom, knowledge, truth, light, peace, love, enlightenment or any other attribute of Reality, because each one is already encoded into our very essence. *It is already there.*

Reality only requires, from the simultaneous changes going on within us, the removal of whatever obstructs our clarity and otherwise prevents our seeing what *never changes*: Reality itself, already there. That is why learning is a matter of unlearning—of removing the misperceptions and illusions which have been drawn in over time and cover Reality, already there.

These insights deeply confirmed what was noted earlier about the spiritual eye when I was three and four years old: we must become again as clear-sighted as little children to see Reality and thereby enter the kingdom of heaven here and now. It confirmed the Buddha's words in the *Lotus Sutra* that who and what we are cannot be extinguished because who and what we are cannot change, or be changed. It confirmed the teaching of Christ that there is everlasting life, and it confirmed my own direct experience of Reality during the near-death: consciousness continues. Only now I knew every aspect of Reality continues, too.

Divine Mother was about to add dramatically to this, however, directing me next to find the home of Krishnamurti, a man whose works I had not read, but whose heart I somehow knew and knew better still for this encounter in the orange grove. I didn't know it then, but he experienced enlightenment in communion with a tree less than half a mile away, and that is where She was taking me.

After obtaining a map to his house, I drove the very little distance and sadly saw a sign declaring the grounds closed for the day. It was impossible, however, not to notice that the entry gate was wide open. I drove in hesitantly, parked, quietly followed the path on foot to the side of the library and then discovered an overwhelming sight. The garden, in smaller dimension, was the *same* scene as the one in my Divine Meditations with Divine Mother:

A graceful grove of trees curved in the same gentle way as the forest had. A bed of beautiful, fragrant roses, by whose scent I had been healed, grew near the grassy clearing. And toward the center I saw, as I had in almost every meditation since She first appeared carrying a lantern in the darkness and we sat down to talk about my children, Divine Mother's *park bench*.

I stood there, stunned.

Divine Mother had led me here to know that this bit of heaven, where I had been given the light in so many meditations, was simultaneously on earth, here, where Krishnamurti had become enlightened. She had been with both of us, as She is always with all of us, here on earth and there on the other side and everywhere in between.

I sat down on the "real" park bench in the garden and felt Divine Mother's Presence extend around me as I began to meditate, going then to the same park bench in the interior garden, and Divine Mother encircled me there, too. We created a living tableau on earth of what was occurring in heaven within, and I simultaneously experienced both in the transparency of the moment ... we were here, but we were there; we were in, but we were out; we were above but we were below.

It was simultaneous cause and effect in action, just like the orange tree, just like Reality. I groped to fathom the double view, and then realized it was impossible. There was, as there is and always will be, only one view to see. And I could see that She and I were *verifying transcendence*: there is no in or out, no above or below, no here or there, no this side or the other side, no now or then, no substance or emptiness, no diversity or consistency, because there is no separation of any kind.

There is only the transparent, never-changing, never-ending union of Spirit. There is only Divine Consciousness. There is only Reality. There is only light. There is only the truth and enlightenment of the Buddha in continuous existence for aeons past and aeons to come. There is only this exalted state of Being.

There is nothing else to see.

I came home from this most remarkable Mother's Day in utter awe. It was especially meaningful to me, too, because of the transparency of the experience. Nothing is transparent without light, and I had waited years to be able to cement the word "transparent" with the only meaning I thought it really had: "through (trans) the parent." This extraordinary view of our unending fusion with Reality had certainly come through One of mine—and it had come through the One with the light.

But even this wasn't all.

The next day, again at Divine Mother's inner urging, I went to the Phoenix Bookstore in Santa Monica and found something unknown to me before: *the Prajnaparamita Sutra*. It is the first of the Mahayana or the higher teachings of the Buddha, and it had been newly translated by Lex Hixon. In fact, he had signed it the day before when I was in Ojai with Her: "For a seeker of truth in Mother Wisdom."

Today Buddhism does not recognize a personal God, yet Divine Mother is nonetheless profoundly recognized in the feminine as Mother Prajnaparamita: the Perfection of Wisdom and the actualization of supreme insight. Further, confirming Her true identity to me as the source of the Buddha's enlightenment, She is unequivocally regarded in this sutra as *the Mother of the Buddhas*.

And She is exquisitely described as I have known Her only to be:

"... a sublime light ... an ever-flowing fountain of incomparable light, and from every conscious being on every plane, she removes the faintest trace of illusory darkness. She leads living beings into her clear light from the blindness and obscurity caused by moral and spiritual impurity as well as by partial or distorted views of Reality. In her alone can we find true refuge. Sublime and excellent are her revelations through all persons of wisdom. She inspires and guides us to seek the safety and certainty of the bright wings of enlightenment. She pours forth her nectar of healing light to those who have made themselves appear blind. She provides the illumination through which all fear and despair can be utterly renounced.

"She clearly and constantly points out the path of wisdom to every conscious being with ... her transmission and empowerment. She is an infinite eye of wisdom [who] dissipates entirely the mental gloom of delusion. Mother Prajnaparamita is total awakeness ... the Perfect Wisdom which never comes into being and therefore never goes out of being. She is known as the Great Mother by those spiritually mature beings who dedicate their mind streams to the liberation and full enlightenment of all that lives. She is the universal benefactress who presents, as a sublime offering to truth, the limitless jewel of all Buddha qualities, the miraculous gem which generates the ten inconceivable powers of a Buddha to elevate living beings into consciousness of their innate Buddha nature.

"She can never be defeated in any way, on any level. She lovingly protects vulnerable conscious beings who cannot protect themselves, gradually generating in them unshakable fearlessness and diamond confidence. She is the perfect antidote to the poisonous view which affirms the cycle of birth and death to be a substantial reality. She is the clear knowledge of the open and transparent mode of being shared by all relative structures and events. Her transcendent knowing never wavers. She is the Perfect Wisdom who gives birthless birth to all Buddhas. And through these sublimely Awakened Ones, it is Mother Prajnaparamita alone who turns the wheel of true teaching."

The word Buddha means "to be awake." There have been many Buddhas or "Awakened Ones," including Christ. Their single aim is to lead us to the enlightenment of Reality by awakening us from the sleep of illusion. But there is no enlightenment or awakening to our innate Buddha nature without the Mother of the Buddhas, without the essence of wisdom, truth and light: Divine Mother.

This is profound and life-altering information about Her, yet how has it escaped our awareness?

As mentioned in Chapter 1, Buddhism—like Christianity and Judaism—came to be governed solely by patriarchal and political powers. Only men were Buddhist priests and only priests were allowed to interpret text, set standards and define accepted doctrine. Complicating matters further, interpretation, standards and doctrine varied from area to area as the Buddha traveled. His teachings passed by word of mouth first in India and then from country to country. As a result, there are literally hundreds of different Buddhist sects in the world, and hundreds of different emphases tempered by various traditions and cultures.

In spite of the Buddha's repeated admonitions in the *Prajnaparamita Sutra* never to forget the Mother—they did. Regardless of His saying "Buddhas and awakened bodhisattvas appear and disappear, whereas the Wisdom Light of Mother Prajnaparamita is always shining"—they ignored Her. Even after He said that the "energy with which to accelerate the spiritual quest of conscious beings can be generated by...indefatigably presenting profound questions and receiving illuminating responses directly from Mother Prajnaparamita"—they didn't ask.

In the *Lotus Sutra*, the Buddha says—twice—"All my doctrines are true and none are false," yet only certain texts were designated worthy of faith by those in authority; they even went so far as to propagate the false belief that women, whom Divine Mother certainly and equally represents, can never achieve enlightenment. That entitlement was exclusively reserved for men, obliterating from consciousness a spiritual place for woman or Mother, no matter how Divine. It wasn't until recent times that Japanese women were even allowed to climb the spiritually sacred Mt. Fuji, let alone function in a meaningful religious capacity.

Just as Judaism claims references to a female God in the Torah signify the state of Israel, not Divine Mother; and just as Christianity claims female references in the Bible describe the Mother Church, not the Mother God, somewhere along the line Buddhism shifted from the Buddha's clear references to an actual Mother to mean the sutras themselves. The wisdom in the sutras became identified with a Buddha nature that did not include Her, instead of being recognized as the essence of the living Mother passed on to all of Her children, whether they are male or female, Buddhist, Christian, Hindu, Jew, or pagan.

These deliberate alterations and omissions have substantially contributed to the spiritual recession we are experiencing in the world today. There is not enough wisdom accessed on the planet to sustain us because the other half of heaven, our direct line to enlightenment, was historically and religiously wiped out. The erasure occurred in Islam's Holy Koran, which otherwise states that "The fruits of paradise come from the mother;" and it occurred in Judaism, despite the fact that Kabbalism, the mystical, secret Judaic system of theosophy, reveals the Reality of "Shekhinah"—the feminine face of God.

Shekhinah is carefully described in the chief text of the Kabbalah, The Zohar, as the Betrothed, the Bride, the Mother, and *Elohim*. "The sole object with which the Holy One, blessed be He, sends man into the world is to know that Jehovah is Elohim"—to know that *He is She, too.*

If that weren't enough, I realized just now, writing this information from the Zohar, something I didn't understand at all before in regard to *how* Divine Mother appeared in the very first meditation carrying the lantern in the darkness. She wore a wedding gown. Divine Mother, our Shekhinah, was dressed *like a bride.*

In the West

As you can see from the above paragraph, the lights still haven't stopping coming on, nor did they stop on that snowy night in Colorado. Calming down from the initial excitement that Divine Mother had been talking to the Buddha, I straightened the covers, fluffed up the pillows and directed my attention for maybe the hundredth time to what Christianity has to offer about Her.

The Bible does say, "Let *us* make man in *our* image, in *our* likeness," (Genesis 1:26) and "So God created man in the image of God, male and *female* he created them." (Genesis 1:27)

There is obviously more than one involved in creation, more than one comprising God, and the identity of the other is female. But the shift to the singular, masculine God is made from that point on; other than the Fifth Commandment, "Honor your father and your mother," which I construe to mean the Father and Mother of the Godhead, there is no other reference to the female God.

Now, Christ had been with me *with* Divine Mother. It's not as if He took me aside and whispered, "Who's *that?*" and I'm just not telling you about it. He unquestioningly accepted Her as Mother God. So, the female imagery must have been overlooked, misplaced, torn up, hidden—*what?* There had to be proof of some kind, didn't there?

A floodlight went on: the Gnostic Gospels. I knew they were written at or just after the time of Christ, buried later for protection, and unearthed after an accidental find in the 1940's. Translations were not made public until the 1970's—not coincidentally, but quite divinely, almost the same year that *"A Course in Miracles,"* exceedingly Gnostic in content, was published.

I did not have the Gnostic texts on hand in my bedroom in Aspen, but I did have a copy of Elaine Pagel's book, *The Gnostic Gospels,* in my bookcase. Purchased years earlier, I had never gotten around to reading it, probably because that snake of an ego went "Hissss!" every time I got near it. In any event, after leaping out of bed to retrieve the book, that is where I read what both Divine Mother and Christ would later verify in Divine Meditation: the true trinity is not "Father, Son and Holy Ghost," as we have been taught, but the completely natural "Father, *Mother,* Son." I literally danced around the room, it was so wonderful to read for the first time what I understood from my experience to be true but had never found acknowledged in print.

Reading on, I learned that as the highly patriarchal Church developed and requisitioned ultimate power over humanity, the Gnostic Gospels specifying the Mother's role as at least the other half of the Godhead were disastrously excluded from the New Testament.

To know She had been intentionally removed was

deeply troubling. The omission had personally caused me years of needless doubt and delay. It obliterated for two millennia the right of Christians—and every seeker of truth, light and intelligence—to the formal, historical information that Divine Mother exists. It led to grossly misleading errors in our teaching, in our learning, in our thinking, in our actions, and in our psychological and spiritual well-being.

With one rewrite, *which humanity not only tolerated but accepted,* the concrete reality of Divine Mother, the Creatrix united in every mind with the Creator, was, in effect, vaporized. But that is what the patriarchy traditionally does: deny to women their individual and/or collective power, strip from consciousness their inherent and just authority that is needed *by the world* for spiritual and physical survival, and not much but a ghost of the original remains. This is exactly what the men in my life had tried doing to me, and you know how I took to that like a duck to a desert.

Women must always resist personal denial or they are consenting to the betrayal of their own *divinity*—and the world's. Because there is only one Mind here, and because "What I think I do to you, I really do to myself" is in constant operation, denial of the female hurts *everyone.*

What was lost in this period of transition cannot be calculated, but it *can* be re-introduced. To that end, the following chapter contains important information gathered from the Gnostic Gospels since that night. If this book were entitled *Divine Mother for Dummies,* it would be categorized as "Technical Stuff." You don't have to read it, but unlike that section in the Dummy series, you'll be a lot happier if you do. It beautifully verifies my heartfelt experiences with Divine Mother, and it confirms everything I have told you about Her.

14

Gnosis

The Greek root "gno" literally means "to know." Gnosis is the process by which we come to know our True Self through direct encounter with God; conversely, we come to know God through direct encounter with our True Self. As this simultaneity occurs, the ego is dissolved and the True Self experiences the enlightened recognition of its real identity as a Being of light, which, male or female, is Joy.

For example, my True Self (the Golden Girl) grew up in direct relationship with God (Divine Mother), and came to know Her as the light. By knowing Her as the light, I came to know I am light, too, and as light, I know that I am Joy.

In Buddhism, the Sanskrit root "bodhi" also means "to know," "to awaken to," one's Buddha nature. This is identical to Gnosis, because it means becoming enlightened to the knowledge that the Reality pervading the universe is inherent in one's being, just as the Reality of one's being is inherent in the universe—something the trip to Ojai proved.

According to the Gnostic texts, Christ taught Gnosticism. In fact, knowing God and knowing who we really are *because* we know God is understood in the West as Christ Consciousness. In the East it is known as Krsna Consciousness and as enlightenment. In essence, they are all one and the same because the highest unifying and revelatory factor in each is the light. And the light, as delving more deeply into the Gnostic Gospels shows, *is* the Mother:

> ... I am immeasurable, ineffable, yet whenever I [wish, I shall] reveal myself of my own accord. ... I am the All, since I [exist in] everyone. ... [I am] the Mother [as well as] the Light.

Indeed, since Divine Mother is the Mother and the light, She could only have given spiritual birth to us *as light.* This is made clear when She says:

> It is I who am the [ ] womb of the entirety, giving birth to the light [ ] in glory.

In *First Thought in Three Forms* (Trimorphic Protennoia, or Thought, Intelligence and Foresight), She further clarifies Her identity, function and presence in the universe and in each one of us:

> [I] am [Protennoia the] Thought that [dwells] in [the Light] ... [She who exists] before the All ... I move in every creature ... I am the Invisible One within the All.

Since Divine Mother is both thought and light, the two combine in Her very Being to produce knowledge. She imparts knowledge to us through telepathic transmission:

> It is I who am the Mother. I speak in many ways; I complete the entirety; acquaintance exists within me—acquaintance with [the] endless. It is I who speak in every creature; and I have been recognized by the entirety. It is I who impart the voice of the sound

into the ears of those who have become ac-
quainted with me, who are Children of the
Light.

I am perception and knowledge, utter-
ing a Voice by means of Thought. [I] am the
real voice.

As we were erroneously taught that the original Trinity was Father, Son, and Holy Ghost, we have been taught
that the Holy Spirit is this Voice. But the Holy Spirit is the
Voice *for* God, functioning in conjunction with, but not as,
God; only Divine Mother, who is God, can ever be the
Voice *of* God. This is a crucial distinction between the two,
and it was almost lost over a single preposition.

She continues (parentheses mine):

I walk uprightly, and those who sleep I
[awaken]. And I am the sight of those who
dwell in sleep (illusions). ... It is I who counsel
those who are hidden (from the truth), since I
know the All that exists in it. ... It is through
Me that Gnosis comes forth.

In other words, it is *through Her* that we awaken to
truth—to the truth which existed, and still does, in each and
every one of us at the point of our creation as spirit before
becoming obscured from consciousness by our descent into
matter. Further, and so importantly, it is *through Her* that we
directly experience Gnosis and, in so doing, expand our current state of awareness to encompass all of Reality. As that
is accomplished, recognition of our first and only real state
of Being is restored as well: one with God.

The Gnostic texts unequivocally reveal the identity
of the Mother as truth and intelligence (the "intelling" factor) which exists with the Father, or Mind. A Gnostic work
entitled *The Great Announcement* states that "a great power,
the Mind of the Universe, which manages all things [ ] is a

male ... and the other ... a great Intelligence ... is a female which produces all things." From the unconscious, where everything originates, emerge "Mind and Truth, and from them, in turn, the Word (logos) and Life." (Valentinus, *The Gospel of Truth*).

A number of Gnostic Gospels refer to God as this dyad comprised of the masculine and feminine, while others report Christ teaching prayer specifically to the Father and Mother, "From Thee, Father, and through Thee, Mother."

In *The Gospel of Thomas*, Christ draws a clear distinction between His own mothers when He says, "my (earthly) mother [gave me death], but [my] true [Mother] gave me life." Mary was His mother on earth, creating and mothering Him in the body which dies, but Divine Mother created and mothered His soul which lives forever.

Divine Mother is referred to in the *Secret Book* by another Gnostic writer as "the image of the invisible, virginal, perfect spirit ... She became the Mother of everything, for she existed before them all."

Two words in the above quotation are, in my mind, of particular importance:

1) "virginal" spirit supports other textual references that Christ's soul was born of spiritual parents: the virgin Mother in this context was Divine Mother, not Mary (the Dead Sea Scrolls reveal that the original word used to portend Mary meant "young maiden," not virgin). This view of spirit born of spirit also explains how Christ could metamorphose from the *Son of Man* on earth (the physical person in a body) into the *Son of God* (the Being of light, the Self without a body) at the point of the resurrection and ascension.

With the same spiritual parents, we are all the physical Son of Man on earth, subject to temptation and redemption, but equally capable of His ascension and resurrection right now. We can manifest the enlightened existence of the Son of God when resurrected from the darkness of illusion into the light of eternal truth and Reality through the living process of Gnosis with Divine Mother. Buddhism shifts

from God to the universal, but the process of enlightenment is exactly the same. The internal encounter with the
light reveals truth and Reality extant within and without.

2) The word "image" in regard to the Mother is *critical* in understanding how She works. In the Gnostic text,
First Thought in Three Forms, She says, "It is I who have im-
parted image unto the entirety." Image was given to all of
us so that we *can* receive truth: "Truth did not come into
the world naked, but it came in types and images. One will
not receive truth in any other way." (*The Gospel of Philip*)

Not only is truth given in the images Divine Mother
transmits to us in dreams and Divine Meditation, but She
Herself appears in Divine Meditation and outside of it in
the image of woman and mother. Marcus, a student of the
Gnostic Valentinus, wrote that a vision "descended upon
him in the form of a woman and expounded to him alone
its own nature, and the origin of things. She said, 'I wish to
show you Truth herself ... so that you may see her without
a veil, and understand her beauty.'"

This is exactly what can and does transpire in a relationship with Divine Mother today. Her light removes the
veil, giving us the clarity to see the beauty of truth, which
is *always* joyous, and to understand this is so by experiencing it. When we see it and experience it, we know She *is* it.
We know Divine Mother is the truth, light, intelligence,
wisdom and knowledge in the universe and in each of us.
We know that by using our birthright of Divine communication with Her, with Her visual voice and audible presence, we can transform our lives and ourselves into Joy.

A real theophany occurs with Her then, for re-union
and communion with Divine Mother simultaneously reveal the True Self. With the True Self comes knowledge of
Reality, knowledge of Joy, and the knowledge that Divine
Mother is a fundamental aspect of our Divine Consciousness, our spiritual psychology and *our actual Being*.

Christ's own role in salvation is not infringed by the
Mother. We have been taught that Christ, Son of both the

Mother and the Father, and brother of all, is the light, the truth, and the way. Certainly He is, but the reason is that the light, the truth, and the way were inherited by Christ as His birthright from the Mother and Father. They are as imprinted in the double helix of His spiritual DNA, as it were, *as they are in our own*.

The difference between Christ and most of us, however, is that He never lost sight of his spiritual identity. He said, "I know where I came from and where I am going," (John 8:14), because He never lost touch with His Mother and Father. He talked to Them, listened to Them, lived in the conscious Reality of Them, and never lost His way. Never having lost it, He remains it: " I am the light of the world. Whoever follows me will never walk in darkness, but will have *the light of life*." (John 8:12)

Whoever follows Christ discovers He is not only the arrow pointing to the Father as the Manager of Reality, but the arrow pointing to the Mother as the Source of truth and light which compose and produce Reality. Christ, the light of the world, points the way to *the light of life, Divine Mother*. That is true whether we have ever recognized Her as the Source of light and truth, the Source of our spiritual experiences and the Source of personal transformation, or not.

Christ is the hand helping bring about our salvation through the recognition of our true identity as children of *both* Parents, for without the Mother we have been allowed only half the true story—and half of God has never fully restored heaven to earth, peace to mind, or light to darkness, because half of God was never intended to accomplish it.

Long ago now, Pia asked me in a meditative state what the end result of these inner experiences would be. In response, Christ appeared in the light for the first time and offered me a dove. I knew that the dove symbolized peace, but I didn't know then that it is also a symbol of the *Mother*. The gift from Christ and the end result of the meditations, then, was and is: *peace obtained through conscious and continuous union with the Mother*.

Christ (Prince of Peace) and the Mother (Source of Peace) work together toward our spiritual liberation and salvation. They join with the Father (Manager of Peace) in the same objective. Anyone who experiences the peace of God through Christ receives it *from* the joint effort of the Trinity, from "the three: Father, Mother and Son," which comprise "the perfect power." (*Secret Book of John*)

In *Trimorphic Protennoia*, the Father speaks:

"I am [the Word] who dwells [in the] ineffable [Voice]. I dwell in undefiled [Light] and a Thought [revealed itself] perceptibly through [the great] Speech of the Mother..."

The actual formation of the Word of God belongs to the Father but the truth and light within the Word are Hers. This is an example of their individual but combined purpose and analogous, say, to a symphony. When listening to a concert, we do not make a point of distinguishing between the music and the mood; we know there is a difference, but we hear the two as one. It is the same here. The influence of the Father and the Mother during Divine Communication cannot be separated any more than music and mood because both exist in tandem.

This may seem a hairline difference, reminiscent of a Buddhist koan, like "How do you unravel a single thread?" The more Divine Mother is directly experienced, however, the clearer the distinction becomes until the one God we have been taught to revere really does unravel to reveal the workings of Two.

One extended look within, an inward turn sincerely taken, shows us clearly now why She *cannot* be reduced to myth, the pagan Goddess, Mother Earth or Mother Nature. She *cannot* be redefined as Mother Mary, although She is the Mother of Mary as much as She is the Mother of us all. She *cannot* be recalculated into an abstract, principle, channeled entity, intuition or figment of the imagination. None of these can be, because here, in the Mind, we *know* Divine Mother Herself. We *know* She is our co-creator, the maternal source and visual voice of truth and light. And we *know* that in the darkest of times, when every single one of us has asked for Mom, what we were really asking for all along is Her.

Another Precious Look

Thousands of years before Christ or Buddha, Divine Mother was known in India, and in Hinduism from which Buddhism developed, as Shakti, Mother God, the supreme reality, the dynamic form of cosmic energy—and She still is. The Ganges River, flowing through India from the top of the Himalayas, is embraced as Mother Ganges not only for its life-giving qualities, but in physical remembrance of Divine Mother: as the body is immersed in its waters in symbolic spiritual cleansing, we may immerse ourselves in the light of the Mother for an actual spiritual cleansing.

The revered Indian philosopher and gnostic, Sri Aurobindo, has written beautifully about Divine Mother in this century by way of a small and slim pink book entitled, *The Mother*:

"The more complete your faith, sincerity and surrender, the more will grace and protection be with you. And when the grace and protection of the Divine Mother are with you, what is there that can touch you or whom need you fear? A little of it even will carry you through all difficulties, obstacles and dangers; surrounded by its full presence you can go securely on your way because it is hers, careless of all menace, unaffected by any hostility, however powerful, whether from this world or from worlds invisible. ... Its touch can turn difficulties into opportunities, failure into success and weakness into unfaltering strength. For the grace of the Divine Mother is the sanction of the Supreme and now or tomorrow its effect is sure, a thing decreed, inevitable and irresistible."

A Course in Miracles

Although I waited expectantly to find it, A *Course in Miracles* says nothing about a female God, something which certainly rattled me when trying to come to terms with both it and Divine Mother before the near-death. The text is *so* overtly male, however, without even a single reference to Mary, that the omission literally creates a yearning for the balance of the Mother.

While setting up desire for Her was the inadvertent accomplishment of patriarch-based religion, I think it was very deliberate in *A Course in Miracles*. With so much information to offer a readership new to its teachings, *A Course in Miracles* could not openly re-introduce Divine Mother without totally befuddling what it so strictly attempts to clarify: the mind. But later, when the mind is so clear as to realize something is missing, it will naturally seek the Mother to fill the void left by Her absence. That is when there is room for additional knowledge, including knowledge about reincarnation. (See Appendix B)

Nonetheless, Divine Mother is always close by in *A Course in Miracles*. For example, a careful reader realizes that there are *two voices* in the text. Christ refers to Himself in the first person "I," for example, yet there are numerous third-person references to "Him" and to "He." The second voice is never identified, even though the writing obviously enlarges to encompass more than one voice by using "We."

I first tripped over the two voices in Divine Meditation with Divine Mother when Christ began speaking to me without being announced. The two energies are very similar and, although I know now who is talking to me without having to ask, I would not always know He had changed places with Her until the third person reference of "She" and/or "We" came into the dialogue.

Since Divine Mother's participation in the transmission of *A Course in Miracles* wasn't known, it wasn't acknowledged, but Her future participation in our lives *is* marked by one caveat the book maintains: it is not the end of all that will be revealed, but rather preparation for what is to come. "God takes the next step." This book is "the next step" She took with me, for you, to rectify the omissions and denial of the past. She has even referred to it as a corollary to *A Course in Miracles* because it proves those teachings, while simultaneously adding to them. In that sense, all of these pages about Her are as much a complement to *A Course in Miracles* as a corollary, and a supplement to all religions in an effort to restore to consciousness what has otherwise been withheld concerning the Reality of the universe:

The truth and light in it have a name, and the name is Divine Mother. The wisdom and voice in it have a face, and the face is Hers.

15

Paradise Lost

The reason Divine Mother could be removed from consciousness goes back much further in time than the patriarchy. In fact, it goes back to our first steps on earth. The story is presented now so when you learn in the next chapter how to meet Her, you will understand why it is a really good idea never to lose sight of Her again.

We all know that "In the beginning, God created the heavens and the earth." What most of us do not know is—*why*? What occurred between the absolute presence of God and the act of genesis to precipitate an entire universe, particularly when every soul was already created and living in cosmic harmony with God before the Biblical account picks up the story with Genesis? (See Appendix C)

Why would anyone turn their back on the splendor and magnificence of a God-given Home, in want of nothing, only to end up driving on a freeway every day or living under one? What purpose could be served by being on earth?

The following version of Genesis 1:1 is taken directly from Divine Mother's original notes. They are pretty old, of course, and some were smudged beyond recognition, but they do illustrate Her sense of humor and provide valid answers by filling in a few gaps. The sheer length answers why the Bible was ever edited; this is, don't forget, *one* verse.

Genesis 1:1

"In the beginning," does not refer to the beginning of eternity. It refers to the beginning of time.

Time began the very instant free will was recognized by the Children of Light as an inherent aspect of Being ... but perceived as a means of independence from God.

The souls accepting this mistaken view of Reality experienced a kind of reverse Big Bang. Instead of consciousness expanding, theirs suddenly seemed to contract. Vision diminished from the immense vista of All to the infinitesimal focus of "me" ... roughly the size of a bumble bee.

To rectify the sudden inequity of now seeing themselves more akin to a pest than to God, and one that scared even them, they threw up a smoke screen of power, called it the ego and would have called it a day but for this:

The ego had reduced their minds from knowing everything to thinking next to nothing, and even that not too well. One of the earliest attempts at thought produced only "Hmm," followed by their first complete sentence, "Now what?"

This precipitated a group decision to find out by abandoning ship altogether, which required the later adoption of the ark as a related motif.

Now, once into this free-fall, it certainly looked like a long fall—and sure enough it was, placing all of these souls in such an unprecedented pickle that God had to do something to save them.

And so it was that God created the heavens as a remembrance of things past, replete with a stairway of stars to light the way Home.

Since time was of the essence, the addition of a celestial platform with a live band had to be abandoned in favor of the quick creation of the earth— simply as a place for them to land.

Ok, so Her handwriting isn't clear about the live band, but I gather Mozart did pick up the intended musical theme when he wrote the Hallelujah Chorus. In any event, Divine Mother's notes are very legible when it comes to the fact that these souls did not ever fall from grace; they fell from *Divine Consciousness, the unifying factor of All.*

To make sure they would not feel entirely like fish out of water, God added a little paradise. Enter Eden: lovely garden setting, rippling rivers, and apples galore. In drops Adam, on goes the body and, to quote Genesis, mankind "became a living being"—a physical entity as opposed to the prior Being of light.

Contrary to Biblical implication, Adam and Eve were not alone. Their son Cain took off after committing the first, but sadly not the last, murder on record, mysteriously finding a wife who just as mysteriously didn't seem to mind about his past. They bore children, and all their male offspring found mates, married, and had children, too.

It is so stunning for us to learn Cain killed anyone, let alone his own brother, that we often neglect to look around for an answer to the highly provocative question dangling in the air of just where any marriage material came from—or, a tad later, how all those faraway towns ever got populated with people. But there is an answer. Many descended *with* Adam, not just from Adam: those caught in the reverse Big Bang, making Adam the Biblical symbol for them all.

Just as Genesis does not mention mankind's first significant error—that hardy dare-devil leap right out of God's arms—neither does it explain the *second* significant error. This occurred when God's very clear directive not to eat the apple fell on unmindful ears. To be fair, though, it must be remembered that these souls, in a strange land and all, were probably still trying to figure out what a weed was, never mind an apple.

The reason behind the admonition not to eat the apple was actually a matter of life—and that thing never heard of before—death. Since no one knew what death was, then what was the harm in ignoring God? After all, ignoring God the first time had produced a pretty good vacation spot. Fascinated by the amenities, they couldn't see that the admonition was important to follow because it required discerning the vital difference between two trees in the garden:

1) the tree of knowledge of good and evil (its botanical name is even longer), and 2) the tree of life.

As Divine Mother explains it, and She should know, "the tree of knowledge of good and evil" was *the tree of illusion posing as knowledge. It was, then, the tree of falsehood and therefore evil. It was the first out-picturing of the ego.*

No soul was to go near it, because good and evil do not exist; they, too, are illusion. What does exist is without qualificaton of any kind: Reality. Reality is represented by the tree of life, which is *the tree of Divine Consciousness, truth, light and eternal life.*

The real choice in Eden, then, was not between good and evil, but between Reality and illusion. The only reason the apple on the tree of knowledge of good and evil even came up was as an opportunity for these souls to use their free will and choose again after their initial, not to mention fateful, leap had landed them so far from Home.

The Bible states "God commanded the man, 'You are free to eat from any tree in the garden; but you must not eat from the tree of knowledge of good and evil, for when you eat of it you will surely die."

It does sound a bit like a commandment, but it was actually an attempt to steer these souls into making the *right* choice this time, because it means, "Believe in illusions and you will surely die," which is to say:

1) Death is an illusion. Believe in it and your mind will die to the Reality of eternal life, truth and light.

2) Being without truth and light is a living death.

3) A living death is being asleep to Reality.

All the above occurred when they ate the apple anyway. Instead of "a Being of light" or even "a living being," they sadly became known in eternal circles as "Those Who Nap."

From the single decision to remain ignorant (i.e., ignore God), the Reality of unity was lost. Taking its place was the illusion of separation, like black and white or good and evil, such disparate concepts they can't be unified. Soon *everything* was perceived by their minds in multiples of two, and since they were asleep, they didn't know which one was even remotely true. And so it was they were unable to recall at all the unqualified Reality of Being they had left behind, not to mention who their Parents were.

Unfortunately, their confusion has been passed on to us today. This graph, which I had to make for myself several times before getting it straight, is what every Being of light needs in order to re-awaken to Reality and make an accurate Parental identification without a line-up.

<u>GOD (+)</u>   **<u>EGO (-)</u>**

Good————————————————Evil
True————————————————False
Truth————————————Illusion
Knowing————Ignorance
Eternity————————Time
Love————————Fear
Light————Dark
Hearing——Deaf
Seeing—Blind
Asleep

With a mind split like the graph, they wobbled back and forth, and then started to slip into the minus category at a pretty rapid rate. Fortunately, a safety net had been provided for them in advance. Like so much else in the Bible, this has not been explained or even pointed out, but it can be found in Genesis 1:3 in the same multiple of two as good and evil. They are often referred to as dualities, polarities or opposites. According to Divine Mother, however, they are *contrasts*: (1) heaven and (2) earth, (1) light and (2) dark, (1) day and (2) night, (1) morning and (2) evening.

The notion behind contrasts was simple. If everyone got tired of earth, darkness, night and evening—especially compared to the alternative *visual aids* of heaven, light, day and morning—maybe they would wake up, realize where they would rather be and return to the *unified* Reality of God. All they had to do was climb back up their life-line, the internal connecting cord of Mother and Father God intertwined within everyone like a spiritual braid of DNA never severed by anyone's fall, and come Home.

Well, everyone *liked* the earth, or said they did, even though they were infinitely smaller here and had to eat hundreds of crooked, spindly things like green beans instead of gazing on a little light to feel full. Later, they took the animals out placidly grazing and minding their own business, cut them up in pieces, placed them on grills fashioned over smokey coals in their caves—and *ate* them.

This kind of thing created a chasm between God and the fallen ones, not on God's side, but on theirs. What with the picking and plucking of food every day, then crouching down to cook it, they rarely remembered to look to God—although, if they did, the air was so full of smoke they could not see much anyway.

Unable to see with any clarity, it was easy to forget about existence before Genesis, before the beginning of time, when there was no need for a beginning, because there was no end; no need for remembering, because there was no forgetting; no need for correction, because there was no error; no need for union, because there was no separation; no need for answers, because there were no questions. There was no need at all, because nothing mattered, and nothing mattered because *there was no matter*.

There existed only the utterly complete state of Being: the shared essence of God that encompassed everything because it denied nothing. All was known but not thought, experienced but not named, and enjoyed but not judged, because each soul was One with the Creators of light, love and truth. Bliss, echoing in the free-flowing and melodious archtones of eternity, comprised Reality—and it still does.

The Consequences

What prevents us from having the clarity to see Reality is the fall from Divine Consciousness that *we all made together*—because 'they' in Divine Mother's version of Genesis is only correct when read as 'we.' No one else contributed to what is found on the planet today, yesterday, or even thousands of years ago. We did it all, with our own free will, and how far have we really come? We still barbecue.

There are elements in life now far worse than rotating a goat on a spit, but each one lets us know the blunder we made by leaving our happy Home and forfeiting paradise, too. We know God can't be thrilled, especially when we have had every second of every day since the beginning of time to change our minds. Our guilt about it begets fear like a chicken the egg, which is why we skedaddle hither and yon like little Henny Pennys, scared the sky is going to fall in. After all, and after All, there has to be *some* retribution for a series of pretty stupendous errors.

Burdened by guilt and fear, hardly anyone is willing to rush Home and face the music. Our parents went ballistic if we came in from a date after curfew. What will this Mom and Dad do if we show up *millions of years* late?

Well, it is ok if we do. Not only does "better late than never" apply, but time is no more real than the guilt, fear or littleness that came with it. God doesn't have a watch. God doesn't even have a calendar. God only has the desire for our return and the open arms to receive us, because we are all the prodigal son: once we wandered away from Home and instead of finding our way back through the contrasting signposts, we got lost in them.

That is all that happened. No guilt, no fear, no big deal. We took a wrong turn off the freeway of God. To get back on, all we have to do is end the contrast of light and dark, day and night, heaven and earth, good and evil, life and death, love and fear. And we can, by using the contrasts for the purpose they were created—as the means of remembering who we really are. Are we dark or light? Day or night? Heaven or earth? Good or evil? Truth or illusion? Love or fear? An ego or a child of God?

Most of us are so stymied by these basic questions that we do need to ask—and ask for the directions Home. In "real" life we do this automatically. We pull into a gas station, ask the attendant for directions and go home. We do not hide in the rest room, thinking, "Ooh, I need to ask for directions, but I don't want anyone to know I'm really lost!" It's exactly the same for re-establishing Divine Consciousness. All we have to do is ask the *attendant*, a word derived from the French *attendre* that literally means "the one who waits"—Divine Mother.

Ask, and You Shall Receive

Confusion about human identity is voiced the same around the world: "Who am I, and why am I here?" Philosophy says the solution to these ancient riddles is "Know yourself," but it doesn't tell us that the solution is not the answer. The answer is to complete the sentence, "Know yourself as God knows you to be."

How? "Ask, and you shall receive."

Most of us do not know how to implement such a simple instruction, nor have we been cautioned to keep a sense of humor about it. "Let there be light," of course, introduced Divine Mother to the earth plane, but the underlying message was always "Lighten up!" Yet that, along with the accurate means of talking directly to God, got lost in all the translations going on around the Tower of Babble and the quibbling over proper pronouns, when we know by now it *does* make a difference if God is referred to as He or She.

All anyone ever mentioned way back when, probably riding camelback in a desert long on heat stroke and short on words, was: "Look to God." That remark had Plotinus, the founder of 3rd-century Neoplatonism, nearly mad with frustration. Not only was God being described as a revengeful sort of *fellow* one would hate to bump into late at night with just a couple of crazy camels for protection, but, "They say only 'Look to God' and do not tell anyone *where* or *how* to look."

Perhaps the authors of the Bible thought the mechanics of Divine Communication so old hat as not to need inclusion. After all, no one in those days had to read a handbook that said, "To keep your donkey alive, please feed it," or "To use a bucket correctly, keep it upright." These were learned by observation. And since inner dialogue with Divine Mother came naturally with the soul, no one scribbled on any stone tablet anywhere just "Pick up the phone."

Now that really would have driven Plotinus mad—how could a call be placed from the center of a person to the center of the universe? Even from present time, reaching out to touch Someone appears too complicated without assistance, and certainly beyond the ability of that little self leaving its smokey cave and roasting goat to traverse the desert with only some shrieking camels for companions.

The little self is unequipped to do much of anything but wander through the sands of time, dragging us along behind, traveling somewhere but going nowhere. In truth, it is this misguided and misguiding self, just as it was mine, that we want to kill off every day—not ourselves and not each other. We correctly desire its death, because this little ego-self stands in the way of the True Self, the pure and innate part of us directly connected to God. Only the True Self knows what the little self does not, without being told and without being taught: "Ask (Divine Mother what you need to know) and you shall receive (the answers)."

Reality Versus Illusion

Divine Mother has said in Divine Meditation, "Seek not enlightenment without, or you will be without enlightenment."

The reason for this advice is that the world is awash with the ego's illusions, misinformation and disinformation, making enlightenment impossible to achieve if looked for outside ourselves. Within, however, lies the true selflessness which leads directly to enlightenment.

"Selflessness" does not mean self-erasure; it means "being without the little self," the ego. As soon as the ego is dissolved, the God-given truths of Reality are automatically restored to our conscious minds, allowing enlightenment to take its natural place. The following chart offers just a few examples of the God-given truths the ego has deliberately distorted in its attempt to keep us from enlightenment.

God	Ego
justice	judgement
independence	separation
acknowledgment	attitude
zero tolerance	anger
assertion	aggression
dignity	justification
privacy	secrecy
refusal	denial
response	reaction
imaging	imagination
confidence	arrogance

correction————————punishment
responsibility————————blame
assessment————————attack
carefree————————careless
faithful————dogmatic
Self-love————vanity
error————————sin

The variations are so subtle, and such a part of the ego's global dissemination of illusion under the guise of truth, that we have erroneously been raised to believe they are correct. Yet they are highly illustrative of the mind split necessary to maintain the simultaneous existence of the ego and God. We are quite capable of bouncing back and forth between each side to meet any situation and then wonder why it is so difficult, and so stressful, to be consistent or set matters straight.

The mind split has other dire consequences. The first error—assessing ourselves as separate from God—produced subsequent mistakes which attached to our light like bits of tarry, sticky tape to an incandescent bulb. Soon other misperceptions drew near, frantic moths to our flame; trapped by the previous mistakes, they compounded them and increased the darkness until we could not see our own light, that of another, or even the greater light of God.

It is as if we once had perfect sight and then arbitrarily decided to wear dark glasses; confident we were seeing more, we were really seeing less. Perceptions skewed. Reality obscured. Error escalated. Our vision diminished so dramatically we might as well have been looking through the bottom of an old mayonnaise jar or, as some might contend, a jar still full, because we began viewing each other not as brothers and sisters, but as enemies, and our own reflection distorted to that of an alien, not a friend.

These distortions and misperceptions were, incredibly, accepted. But following another ego-directive—to reverse ourselves from big to small—did not sit nearly as well. By the time we had reduced ourselves to little cave-folk, we weren't really out there clubbing each other on the head out of territorial instinct over property rights; we were just sick and tired of having to deal with one more living reminder of the littleness we had made of ourselves. Shrink-wrapping a soul the size of the universe to make it conform to a human body was like washing our only clothes in hot water and then spending eternity in attire tailored to a tot.

It didn't fit right.

The ego, as usual, threw up its tiny hands. It had no solution to this situation destined to keep us knee-high to a camel, but then neither did we. With the phone to God off the hook, we were helpless in putting this historical time-frame to use other than expanding our self-concept of little to really irate.

God did not fare any better during this era, one peculiarly viewed by historians as being naturally aggressive when there was nothing natural about it. Nor was it natural when, deluded by so many mistaken choices, we gave Reality one last kick in the pants by deciding we were not created in God's image after all—God was created in ours. As a result, poor old God, Who had done nothing to merit such a hideous character assassination, metamorphosed through the eyes of our oh-so-highly evolved tribal consciousness into a wrathful, angry creature, too.

The beauty of this ego-rewrite was that God could be blamed for anything. We could hit each other over the head any old time, especially if one of out little neighbors got out of line by getting big again, and not even have to feel guilty about it. After all, what with plagues and famines, God had been hitting us since Eden. It was far easier to pin it all on God than realize that any disaster (which literally means "removed from the stars," removed from the light) marked the earth's intolerance of our destructive thinking, a not-so-subtle notice that we needed to change—oh, everything.

Gray-matter was in such short supply, however, that lots of things were easy to accept then. With the ego-finger pointed at what it considered the betrayal of Eve, it only stood to reason God must be a man, when with all that crazy club work going on, we hardly had reasoning down pat. Yet when cranial capacity increased, our ability to reason didn't improve much. By the time Christ, the Son of God, came into the world, no one even wondered, "Gee, how did such a Mean Guy have such a Nice Kid?"

No, we just plunged along, dented head first, for another two thousand years to this very day where the time-honored practice continues. Illusions adhere to the tarry, sticky tape of other illusions already in place, ill-prescribed lenses distort our vision, and as painful as it is, we live out the lie that we are who we are not. Every single life is consumed with the errors of the ego, and we watch them played out now on another kind of tape, projected through another kind of lens, on the nightly news, just as we have always projected them onto a neutral world.

We are *not* unable when it comes to exchanging illusion for truth, but we are unenlightened about it. Enlightenment is a state of consciousness well within the reach of each individual because the word simply and literally means "being in the light." It also means *staying* in the light, but Divine Mother, as you have noticed, will personally see to it that we do. Considering our past as miniatures, some "enlargement" might be in order, too. Fortunately, the simultaneity inherent in cause and effect means that both occur *at the same time*: when enlightenment cancels out the reverse Big Bang, and it does, we are automatically ballooned back into our original, expanding state of Being.

To accomplish this here and now, we need only turn from the television or computer screen to focus on that from which the two were developed: the panoramic field of vision of our own internal mind where Divine Mother and Divine Consciousness await our return. Exactly how to do that, and how the process differs from conventional meditation and prayer, is detailed next, step by step.

16

Paradise Regained: Divine Meditation

The following outline is a preview of the material in this chapter and can be used later as a quick reference for Divine Meditation on your own.

Divine Meditation
Step by Step

1. **Making the Call**
    a. dial the number
    b. the light
    c. the dark
    d. ask for protection
    e. ask for Divine Mother

2. **Staying on the Line**
    a. *do not* hang up
    b. be patient
    c. the prospect of mediation

3. The Importance of the Image
  a. a scene materializes
  b. receiving images
  c. look and listen
  d. we are not alone here

4. The Impact of the Image
  a. numinosity
  b. cleansing
  c. understanding
  d. new views and information
  e. mediation and renewal

5. The Conversation
  a. asking questions
  b. expressing feelings
  c. hiding nothing
  d. the answers in symbols,
      words and telepathy

6. Back in the "Real" World
  a. after-glow
  b. acknowledge the truth
  c. don't fight it
  d. remember it
  e. use it

The details are next so you will always know what to do and what to expect. Absorbing this information now will literally save you years of trial and error on your own.

1. Making the Call

We begin by ignoring every ego-delay that suddenly comes to mind—and it will, like writing a letter to Aunt Alice we put off for seven years but must answer this very minute; cleaning out the attic when we don't even have an attic, or learning how to skip to my lou. Well, someone did it in the second grade. Now is as good a time as any, isn't it?

No.

We have to sit in a quiet place, close our eyes, and key in to the invisible lines of Divine Communication by using the original telephone: telepathy. We know the number by heart because it is written there, so we dial directly by counting from 10 to 1, going deeper and deeper to still the mind and call up a clear screen in front of the third eye.

If the light first appearing on the screen of our mind looks like fireworks—a bouncing, dazzling display of erratic little lights—don't worry, the "1812 Overture" is not going to be played in your head. Just continue to relax, dial down again (repeatedly, if necessary) until the light calms down, too, and begins to coalesce.

Now, the ego has special radar to scout out anything as preposterous to its mind as peace. The second its sensors pick up even the slightest hint of calm, alarms go off, locks go on, and blockades to the light in the form of even more distracting thoughts shoot out of nowhere. "Oh, no, I forgot to *mail* the letter to Aunt Alice!" or "Oh, Stevie Snyder skipped to my lou in the second grade. Jean Enloe did, too. How did that go? Fly's in the buttermilk, shoo fly shoo, fly's in the buttermilk, shoo fly shoo, fly's..." If we actually manage to get that tune out of our head, the ego will provide something impossible to ignore, like where we hid a $100 bill five years ago. We'll want to jump up and go spend it, totally forgetting what we came here to do, when chances are, since the ego had a say in it, the bill will be counterfeit.

Distraction during this stage is one of the oldest ego tricks in the book—and usually the most effective. If we are tempted to fall for it, and we will be in the beginning, here is the antidote: just remember that this ploy is exactly what Nixon used so no one would find out about Watergate. It is called a cover-up, and it is covering up the truth. If we want that kind of devious mentality running our mind like it ran the country, ok, but this little realization is usually enough to return immediate focus to the task at hand.

We will know the number is going through when the light, although still moving, becomes cohesive. At this point the light can be any color or mixture of colors with varying degrees of clarity. The color and condition of the light are entirely dependent on our current state of mind and awareness, how much negativity has come in just that day, and/or the area to be worked on. If we hit a neighbor during a spat over the oleander bushes the day before, it is going to be pretty dark, but if we spent the day praying for peace in the world and gratitude for everything in it, the light is going to be just pretty. If we have neither attacked anyone nor taken a stab at sainthood, it will be somewhere in between.

I have seen transparent blues (pure communication/ Divine Mother), glass greens (health/growth) and clear yellow (pure intellect) centered in the darkness. There was a long period when the light was a sparkling golden lavender (spiritual sight), which was followed by years of a gorgeous golden, periwinkle blue: the gold of enlightenment, the blue of Divine Mother and the rosy hues of love.

Although frequently flooded with the blue of Divine Mother as She emphasizes a particular point, a soft gold is the primary color now, followed by the white-gold writing of truth and light against a dark background.

Gold is the highest metaphysical color. It is also the color of the light of Christ Consciousness, enlightenment, and soul power. In addition, gold was the goal of alchemical practices which attempted to transmute ordinary metals into gold; gold symbolized then, as it does now, transformation of the common mortal into the immortal Being.

Gold has another meaning as well. It is what we seek at the end of the rainbow, a quest Divine Mother explains in a unique way: the color spectrum of light represented by the rainbow is what we are to follow *spiritually* to reach the golden light of enlightenment. The gold is not found at the right or left end of the rainbow as it touches the earth, but at the *summit end of the rainbow.* We are to travel spiritually up through the various colors to *that* end of the rainbow to find the pot of gold: our own enlightenment.

There are reasons *not* to compare the colors or intensity of color you receive to my color scheme or anyone else's.

1. The order of the colors will vary depending on (a) the most critical need, (b) the chakra related to that need, and (c) the color required to correct it. If the heart chakra, for example, needs more green, but blue already exists in abundance, the predominant infusion will be yellow. Divine Mother knows the order of the colors necessary for each of us individually and the order must be left to Her.

2. Just as a plant taken from the shade and placed in direct or intense sunlight will die from the exposure, it is to our benefit to trust the degree of light Divine Mother sends at any point as perfect for us at that moment. We are seeking inner sight, but that doesn't mean it will happen overnight, and no one wants to be so exuberant for it that they are *blinded* by the light.

As for the degree of darkness mingling with the light or surrounding it, is important to remember the following.

1. If we have been even unconsciously affected by negative energy in our surroundings, there may be more darkness on any given day than anyone would like.

Divine Meditation is a life-long process because life is long on illusion. Illusion is present in virtually every mind on the planet. Buddha and Christ constantly meditated, not just for guidance or assistance, but to clear out any contamination from the darkness in Their environment—and so must we.

2. As much as we are attempting to dissolve it, darkness is not bad. A certain amount is required in order to create a contrast so the light can be seen.

Darkness is a catalyst in the alchemy of change. Photographic negatives, for example, require a "darkroom" before they can be exposed to the light, or the pictures will not materialize. Similarly, a caterpillar is encased in the darkness of its own cocoon before it can be transformed into a butterfly.

Darkness can also be an impetus into the light. It may be used, as it was in my case, as a positive charge, rather than the negative we perceive it to be.

3. The tarry, sticky tape of misperceptions is dense. That density often determines how much light we are able to perceive and receive. As the misperceptions are removed by the light, the density is reduced, allowing for greater clarity of color.

No matter how long we have practiced Divine Meditation, the light is initially amorphous during each encounter, softly rolling and in constant motion. It may be preceded by a small, bright white star like one seen in a clear night sky, or by a pair of closed eyes; these are our own eyes, closing in recognition of the opening of the third eye of inner sight. The amorphous mass of light will always follow, however, so we will wait for it now—and wait for it to slow down. As it does, we will notice from our interior view that it is rolling counterclockwise on the screen of our mind in calming, rhythmic waves as if pushed by an invisible windshield wiper. If the light is not turning in the correct direction, we can "urge" it the right way by using a "push" of personal will. The same applies if individual chakras appear.

It is important now to ask for holy protection from Divine Mother and any other spiritual presence with whom we feel close—or, as my son Linc used to say when he was little and couldn't remember every name, "Divine Mother, and all you other Folks." The request guarantees protection from the many fearful forms we may make of darkness, any negative content we may (erroneously) anticipate, and it keeps us secure in the face of any personal vulnerability that may consciously or unconsciously exist.

Then we simply ask to talk to Divine Mother.

2. Staying on the Line

Having asked for Divine Mother, we will now be put on hold. I doubt there is a Divine Switchboard with an operator out to lunch, but it really can feel like that. Still, we will patiently stay on the line—and stay very focused.

Even though there is no Muzak, we do not want to start wondering about our next dentist appointment as we might during a traditional delay on the phone. We do not want to space out and drift around the universe just because we are there. We do not want to try to get centered (that automatically happens), gain wisdom from a word or contemplate the void as in other meditative practices, and last but not least, we *do not* want to hang up as in prayer.

How many times have we all jumped the prayer gun, thinking Someone was listening, and said, "Oh, God! I need the rent money a week on Tuesday or I'll be evicted!" then slammed down the phone and run away—to wash the car or do the dishes, half-hoping money will mystically hop out of the soap-suds like silver dollars from a slot machine?

If we had just hung around at the point we hung up, we would have gotten a real answer about our situation then and there. Indeed, the resolution of *any* problem is received here, because *an accurate and immediate interior response* is one of the major differences between Divine Meditation and prayer, supplication, day-dreaming, conventional meditation, and even thinking.

The reason a direct answer can occur is that Divine Meditation offers the opportunity for *direct mediation.* It is not the place where nothing happens, but where everything happens. It is not the place of "Those Who Nap" as in Eden, but of the vibrantly awake. It is not the place of sedentary emptiness but of vital activity—because this is the place where all is made known. This is where the real resolution of any problem *takes* place. Resolution literally means "to solve again." A problem from the near or far distant past has come into the present to be solved again because we didn't do it right the first time. This is no cause for alarm. The repeat appearance means Divine Mother can now help us handle it correctly, thereby handling it for all time. *Generally, anything internally handled with Her will not have to be handled externally; the outer environment conforms itself to the changes made within.*

3.   The Importance of the Image
We can be certain the connection has been made when something, generally a scene, begins to materialize spontaneously on the screen of our mind. It may be anything from a flower garden, an orchard of blossoming fruit trees, the mountains in spring or the summer seas, to the interior of a classroom, a library or a home. It may be a place from the past, the future, or one we have never seen before.

No matter what or where the scene is, remember we were given the ability to receive images—*not* the ego's interpretation of imagine as in "make up"—for the very purpose of receiving the *truth* here. Truth will be given to us within the context of the scene; every aspect of the scene will have meaning; Divine Mother always knows the best ones to bring up for us *individually*, and we will understand it all either immediately or over time.

Now, if nothing should happen at this point, we can continue to wait, or look to the far right side and give ourselves a visual third-eye boost over the darkness, like jumping a fence. A scene, image or words will appear, and we just move it to the center of the screen of our mind.

Depending on our particular needs, and on our readiness, Divine Mother may not initially appear. She may send an emissary in Her place, a spiritual representative who will ensure a smooth reunion with Her by resolving certain conditions or issues beforehand. If it is someone we know and trust, living or deceased, fine. If not, it is important to ask their name and purpose for three reasons. 1) We don't talk to strangers in "real" life and we shouldn't here. Not everyone on this side or the other side always has our welfare at heart. 2) We don't often share our inner thoughts and feelings with someone we have just met and we needn't here, either. 3) It takes time to establish a trusting relationship, even with Divine Mother. The more we know whoever has come, the more comfortable and confident we will be.

Once, when first working with Pia before the return of Divine Mother, I meditated to meet my personal guide. It turned out his name was Paolo, and he had come to guide me in relationships. Paolo was a very handsome, attractive soul with whom, he said, I had spent many Portuguese seafaring lifetimes. All of the imagery that appeared spontaneously with him related to the sea.

Meeting with him again at home that night in meditation, he took me to a beautiful lighthouse with a great beacon of light. We went up a winding staircase, surrounded by glass, to a landing. Paolo then suddenly turned and *kicked* me down the stairs; I went spiraling to the bottom. Shocked, I looked up in the meditation and asked, "What did you do that for!" He answered, "Because it's exactly what you let men do to you."

Pia was appalled by this account at the next class and told me that he was not a good spirit; they are always kind and supportive. There were only a few times Pia wasn't correct and this was one of them. When the scenario was explained, however, she understood:

Even after Michel, the tendency to let men "kick me around," emotionally and mentally, persisted. I had just never put it in those terms, making Paolo's kick the most potent, graphic and direct form in which much-needed information could be presented and received. It was so clear it was impossible to miss and that *was* kind and supportive.

Once it was so obvious, we dealt with it. Paolo and I spent many subsequent evenings (which also meant "evening" as in balancing, setting aright, smoothing) in a house beneath the sea (beneath what is seen by the physical eye, deep in the third eye of spiritual sight). We sat together on the couch, a fire in the fireplace, his arms around me. All he did was love me, offering a first-hand experience of what a loving relationship is, because I could no longer remember. Learning to love and be loved opened the pathways for reciprocal love to flow between Divine Mother and me.

Now, as it turned out, Paolo had added a surprise in the form of the lighthouse with the beacon. It did not just mean where I could find the light housed within myself. Alex lived on Beacon Lane—only I didn't know that then; I hadn't met him yet. And it would be for Alex and me, too, as well as for the resolution of our joint negative karma, that it was so important for me to learn what it means to love and be loved, to cherish and uphold. We had hurt each other in many ways over various past lives and would have to learn these positive ways of avoiding old patterns.

Yet there is even more significance to Paolo. 14 *years* after meeting him, and during one of those after-the-event confirmations, I learned from a friend that Paolo is an Ascended Master whose function is "to teach us how to love."

With such a richness of information from a single scene as just this one with Paolo, we would be in great error to view what occurs in Divine Meditation as imaginary, unreal or insignificant. I made that mistake before meeting Divine Mother directly. She appeared as a fairy Godmother and I thought, "I'm making this up. No one has a fairy God-mother," but we all do, She is one, so if anything is not clear immediately, it will be. Words, which are also symbols, may be seen or heard in the form of sentences, paragraphs or entire conversations. They too will be verified in time.

So for the moment let's just accept what we are given and not disregard it as nonsense or fantasy. We are out of body consciousness at this point, out of the ego's domain, out of the part of the mind that *can* fantasize. The little self ceases to exist now, as do its spin-offs of time, space and illusion. This means we are experiencing everything through the True Self and the light of Divine Mother.

4. The Impact of the Image

If Divine Mother does not appear at first, the images are still *from Her*. Each one is infused with Her light, truth and intelligence. This is luminosity, the essence of Divine Mother coming "in types and images" as noted in the Gnostic Gospels—and it is the profound, dynamic, vital spiritual energy referred to by Carl Jung, an advocate of the Great Mother, as *numinosity*.

Like Divine Mother, numinosity must be *experienced* to be known. Pure mental and emotional energies combine with the Divine power of light, truth and intelligence in the images to dislodge and wash away all the distorting, sticky grime of illusion in our minds. Numinosity accomplishes *on impact* the inner cleansing we unconsciously sought before by running out to wash the car or the dishes, up to our arms in soapsuds. It is manifested incrementally according to our capacity to receive it and leads to enlightenment simply *by* experiencing it. In other words, *it does the work for us.*

The numinous impact is so critical, it is very important to remember that the words and images Divine Mother chose for me during the Divine Meditations included in this book were all *empowered by numinosity*. Reading them without the benefit of experiencing the numinosity within them is *not* to know their profound ability to transform.

Because that is true, Divine Meditation must be experienced personally to receive its full effect. It is impossible for anyone else ever to do it for us. In the same way that we must dream our own dreams and be awakened by them, our consciousness is awakened by the vivid power of numinosity occurring in Divine Meditation. Even then the effects of numinosity are more powerful in Divine Meditation than in dreams because there is no subconscious ego at work to distort the images working their way up from the unconscious to the conscious mind.

Whether it seems so or not, numinosity always occurs in Divine Meditation. Until you know it for yourself, please trust me on this; I did enough doubting for all of us. Some illusions, like my subconscious (ego) thought of equating love with being kicked around, are eliminated with the first jolt of recognition, but others require the deeper cleansing and purification of sustained and repeated clarity.

For example, if being hit on the head to accept the light in the near-death seems a bit much, it is nothing compared to how many times Divine Mother had to say, "Love more!" before Alex came close to getting a fair shake—and She did not just mean love him more. She meant love myself more, and She stayed on that line and only that line until I decided to get off my ego-pedestal and ask, *"How?"* which certainly opened up a whole new area of conversation.

In all of these various ways, the truth and the light act like spiritual Windex. We can see more clearly through the windshield of our mind after using it once, but a perfect view may require additional applications depending on the depth of the dirt. Pure sunlight then streams in and we can finally see where we are going. If it is the right way, we can continue in full confidence. If not, we can change direction.

In addition to many other benefits of Divine Meditation, new views are developed from the direct knowledge inherent in each of the symbols and images. For example, at the end of 1990 in Colorado, Divine Mother took me into a Divine Meditation that turned out to be a metaphor of the earlier fight for freedom from the ego, the near-death, the awakening, *and* what would be coming next:

> It was a great struggle for me to swim upward through a thick fog. I couldn't see an inch ahead, but I would not give up. I finally broke through the fog, bobbing up suddenly, and surfaced in the still, clear and utterly quiet universe. There were planets, stars and endless space. I twirled around in the joy of being free, dancing in the light.
>
> My attention was then focused back on the fog of illusion from which I had come. I saw that it covered the earth. In a very somber moment, I was told that I had to re-enter the fog. I had to help pull the next person out.

I returned to California shortly after this meditation, having no idea that the person I had to help pull out of the fog of illusion was Alex. We had not yet had time together to correct our relationship, but I could tell just from the first phone conversation in Los Angeles that something was terribly wrong; he didn't sound himself.

After the near-death, Alex said to me, as did others, "I didn't know what to do for you." I vowed at that time never to be in a similar position when it came to helping people, nor would I ever have to be; we can always ask Divine Mother *exactly* what to do.

So, deeply concerned about Alex, I followed Divine Mother's guidance to chant for him, which turned out to be from the heart of my soul. The need to help him *that instant, with no time to lose,* intensified to such an extent, I literally demanded of the universe to give over to him every single benefit I may ever have earned for myself, past, present or future. This was a "transfer of benefits" I didn't know even had a name, but *had* to make because I loved him so much.

At the most intense point of the chanting, the entire altar—symbol of *altering* conditions—ignited through the third eye into pure gold light. I had never seen such a thing. It was my first *conscious* experience of enlightenment, of Being light and Being in the light, of the environment around me powerfully and profusely reflecting back the light I was offering Alex. I wasn't rich, I wasn't a doctor—I had nothing to give to him *but* the light.

Alex had no idea at the time that he was close to dying, nor did I know that was the reason to demand the light. As it happened, the probem was found suddenly, he was operated on just as suddenly, and not wanting to alarm me, I was not told anything until it was over. Without demanding the benefits and the light exactly when I did, I don't think Alex would have survived. Later on, wanting to know if that were true, I meditated to ask Divine Mother and She said, "You are incorrect to believe otherwise."

She had much to say about the long-term prognosis for Alex after the operation—but I stalled finding out what it might be; I didn't want to meditate only to discover that death might still be his fate. Because of my reluctance, Divine Mother kindly and quietly came to me one evening:

> I was alone in the bathroom when the light changed, shifting to a soft, brief radiance of pink indicating Divine Mother's presence and marking Her desire to be heard. I looked to the right of the third-eye and, in the ethers of that interior, a note card came toward me. Inside it said, "Please come talk to Me."
>
> Ready or not. I went into the den and relaxed into meditation somehow, knowing this would be the most personally valuable information I had ever received. I turned on the tape recorder and She began:
>
> "Alex loves you so, dear, so dearly that the trees shine forth with his love."

The vision She shows me is that no matter where I look and there is light, there is Alex; there is love. I tell Her, "I am so happy," to know this; it is such vitality, such life.

The interior scene gradually changes to a place that is very special to Alex and me. He walks toward me now, lifting me up into the sunlight and looking me straight in the eyes with so much joy and love.

Divine Mother says, "You have a mission together. Please believe Me when I say so, that you are to love one another truly, without affectation, without fear, with enormous compassion. ... You are not to lose your way again from each other, but walk steadfastly together toward the light of love, manifesting it daily in your lives and creating the light of heaven on earth. Believe Me, please, that this mission is not accidental, or obtrusive, but demanded by your insistent souls to recover the harmony of the earth. But mark my words, this will not be easy, for you chose the rocky road to manifest the splendor of the earth in truth. Always walk together now. That is your destiny. Keep faith in each other now and always as one in spirit and Christ/Buddha light of eternity/eternal love and devotion. ... All signs and conditions point your way to peace, children, together, not alone anymore. Freedom is your desire and so be it."

I ask, "How?"

"Because you will it so together, not alone anymore. Side by side by side. [Alex and I walk *side* by *side* with Divine Mother at our *side*.] There is no time, place or space to prevent its occurence. The time is now and so be it. No question."

Listening to it again, I realized how beautifully She had answered my deepest, unspoken question whether he would live or not by disclosing what would happen for us and with us in the future. The meditation was so precious, the joy and encouragement so valuable, and the truth such an incomparable relief when all appearances gave every indication to the contrary, that I slept with the little tape recorder like a baby in my arms, over my heart, and did not move all night.

I had complete faith in what Divine Mother said, and Her words proved accurate. Because of that, think for a moment about the despair, grief, fear, uncertainty and concern I *never* had to experience in this situation. Further, but far less important, the accrued benefits offered to Alex were not denied to me. Because of my sincerity in giving them, they were doubled by Divine Mother to encompass Alex, and he healed beautifully—in so many ways.

Of course people do die, unexpectedly and often tragically in our view, but we can understand *why* the death occurred by talking with Divine Mother. That kind of information induces peace of mind in which there can be no tragedy, grief, fear, uncertainty or concern. The comfort, wisdom and grace of Divine Mother, Her unfailing knowledge in all matters, and the presence of other beneficent Beings, are here to *prevent* pain by enlightening us to the reasons behind everything that happens.

So please know that in one way or another the illusions of fear, suffering, illness, and even death can always be transposed into the truth of understanding, peace, health, joy, and the recognition of eternal life—if we will only meditate and receive what is here *for the asking*.

Information of every kind increases in Divine Meditation as we become ethically and emotionally responsible for it. This is very high-powered stuff. No one puts the keys to a Lamborghini in the hands of someone without a license, so it is to our advantage to meditate as often and as honestly as possible.

5. The Conversation

The conversation is begun by saying hello . If there is not a response initially, and for those first trying that may be the case, ask to speak with someone else or take time to explore the setting. There is a great deal of information in this alone and someone else may be waiting in another area.

Once the dialogue begins, it is important to ask questions, express fears, concerns or problems freely and hide *nothing*. Unlike the police after a confession, these Folks will still love us. In addition, acknowledging our emotions here is very liberating. If we feel terrible, *we need to say so, no matter how long we have been meditating and no matter what the subject.* Many times I was concerned about something or another but Divine Mother would make one funny comment that completely dissolved my feelings about it. This one change in my perception—the effect of Her ability to "lighten up" any matter—can often change the situation in real life, too. Her humor removes my seriousness, I no longer perceive the situation as a problem and it dissolves, too. Because of Her, I don't compound the situation, or make real what didn't even exist to begin with, by taking any action on it.

As the conversation progresses, we can calmly allow the unfolding of scenes, images and action without interfering; Divine Mother can be trusted to do what needs to be done, because only Higher Intelligence knows what that is. As smart as we are, we *do not* have access to all the pieces in the puzzle of our life; knowledge of what we need to learn; awareness of every psychological stance on a given problem; how another person thinks or what they will do—but Divine Mother does, and that makes Her guidance unerring and extremely effective.

Initially there may not seem to be an abundance of information, but there is. It is wise to put tape to good use now by recording every aspect as it occurs, because it will have meaning. In addition, misplacing a single word or forgetting a symbol can not only alter the meaning, but, if given the opportunity, the ego will do its best to recollect it incorrectly for us once the meditation is over.

Here is an example of the need for accuracy.

Once, Divine Mother took me into a past-life scene in India. I could see myself as an extremely happy little boy riding down a dusty dirt road in the country on the back of an elephant with an upturned trunk. Divine Mother sat on the side of the road and pointed out how She loved me as that child as much as I loved my own boys. From this perspective, I understood for the first time the depth of Her love for me. She said that my current lifetime was similar to this one and could be summed up as "Victory in happiness."

It wasn't possible to transcribe the tape until the next day. In that short amount of time, Divine Mother's words had been returned to my mind as "Happiness in victory," quite an alteration of the true intent. I am dyslexic like my sons, something that typically signifies a larger right brain hemisphere. While this facilitates Divine Meditation—*such* good news for dyslexics, who can have trouble with worldly things from spelling to shoe-tying—it can and does tend to reverse the content during recall. Tape-recording, then, is mandatory for a variety of reasons.

6. Back in the "Real" World

After the thank-yous and goodbys have been said, attention is consciously brought back to the present and the receiver is placed back on the phone by opening our eyes. Anyone seeing the glow in them would think we had just made love—and by re-uniting with truth and light, we have. So we can take these after-moments to rest in the warmth, comfort and security. These are the feelings that will initially motivate us to return to the interior universe, but they will eventually become the predominant sensations in our life as the truth and light within are turned inside out and a whole new world begins: when our mind is cared for by Divine Mother, there is only peace.

When the Buddha said in the *Lotus Sutra* that He had

attained enlightenment in the far distant past, He spoke for each one of us; we were all created then as light, and as light, *direct contact with God* is our Divine right.

There is no real abyss to separate us from God because no real fall took place; we just turned from the light in our own minds. But turning to it now, to communicate with Her ourselves, ultimately reveals our true identity as Beings of light, just as it reveals the true meaning of enlightenment: Being in the light. Unlike our birth into eternity in Heaven or our birth into time in Eden, however, we will come to value what we did not value then: Divine Consciousness. And we will value it because we will have at last an objective, not subjective, knowledge of Reality.

Not everyone becomes an instant believer overnight. The ego tries to take back control by finding ways to convince us that what we experienced in Divine Meditation is untrue. Once, a woman I know asked if a certain man would help get her project going. Divine Mother answered yes, but the woman's ego decided this meant he would get it "up and going." He quickly returned her work and the woman's ego as quickly judged Divine Mother wrong. In truth, however, the man was helpful: he forced the woman to move on to someone she hadn't considered—and he got it up *and* going.

Regardless of the initial reaction, what we learn from Divine Mother will prove correct and in our best interest if followed because this truly is "our daily bread," the spiritual sustenance of unalterable truth and Reality we all need each day for psychological survival in our otherwise highy unstable world of illusion.

We will soon become as accustomed to Her as we are now to breathing, finding Divine Mother the Source of enlightenment, kindness and love our heart and soul have always sought. She will guide our affairs, thoughts and feelings into alignment with the peace of light, truth and knowledge until one day that is our only state of mind. Then we will forget there ever was an ego—just as we once forgot the Reality of Divine Mother God.

17

Karma

Karma, particularly our negative karma, will come up in Divine Meditation. That is good news, because that is where it can most easily be resolved. The bad news is that while the East has always been savvy about karma, we in the West threw off that yoke from the past like a straightjacket. A rebellious lot, we don't go back, we go forward; we don't go East, we "Go West, young man!" and we certainly don't go within—we go to outer space.

Almost every move we make is away, from *ourselves*, which is why negative karma persists lifetime after lifetime; why it must come up for interior resolution, and why, after going to great lengths to avoid this invisible source of every calamity in our lives, we are shocked when it shows up anyway, generally with the grace of a detonated bomb. We suffer then over the appalling difference between how things are and how they should be, asking, "How could God let this happen?" when the correct question is, *"How could we?"*

Whether we want to throw it off like a yoke from the past, rebel against it, deny it, delay it or hide behind it, our conscious attention needs to be on it, because not taking personal responsibility for all the conditions in our lives is *the* reason for our continuing unhappiness: when we refuse to be responsible, we refuse to do the spiritual homework that will liberate us into genuine joy.

Instead, and especially when karmic problems jump from a personal to local, national or global level, we fall back on Christ's words, "Let him who is without sin cast the first stone." The ego misinterpreted this long ago to mean we are each so guilty that no one has the moral right to step forward to fix anything, whether it pertains to another person, a situation or ourselves. If sin were a cement we could not escape, the ego might have a case, but Christ's intent was encouragement: if we pursue self-examination and correct the sin in ourselves first, we will, by example and by the release of fundamental truth in our lives, assist others in correcting their sin, freeing us *both*. And correction is easy when we understand that sin is simply an archaic archery term meaning to "miss the mark," i.e. make a mistake; the negative karma in our lives, in another's, or in the world is only *erasable error*. It is no more permanent than a pencil mark.

Divine Mother says that the good we do multiplies by three into perpetuity, but error is returned to us *ten times harder each time* until we erase it by correcting it.

This return of error, which can strike with the sudden severity of an electrical storm, is known as negative karma. The advantage of its ten-fold intensity is that the sheer force will make us seek and implement a correction. Once we do, the negative karma has no reason to return. The rain stops, dark clouds vanish, and blue skies shower us with peace.

If we believe the ego's version of error, however, correction doesn't enter our head as we seek shelter, not a solution, at the first sign of darkening clouds. The ego supports that reaction because it doesn't want us to know that the storm will only become ten times stronger in the future and revisit us in torrential if not hurricanic proportion.

What avoiding karmic solutions means overall is exemplified by a man named Monty. He recently had an explosive confrontation with the managers of his apartment building, an unconscionable group known to ignore legitimate complaints. The managers were in error, but instead of reporting them to the owners, Monty said he had forgiven the management and would do nothing.

Forgiveness is invariably appropriate, but *forgiveness does not mean tolerance.* By failing to hold the managers accountable, they were free to continue their dictatorial ways, and they have. Every time an error is *tolerated by* forgiveness rather than *corrected with* forgiveness it will occur again. This is the same mistake we make with our own weaknesses, as well as those of friends, neighbors, governments, businesses, institutions, and entire countries.

But this is the crux of the story:

Monty's decision to overlook the incident wasn't due to the altruism he professed, but because his behavior as an employee of another company is *identical* to that of the managers. The ego's version of "Let him who is without sin cast the first stone," was certainly at play here, but beneath that was an even more insidious ego ploy—Monty didn't want anyone at work to report him; therefore he wouldn't report the managers. He did not have the personal integrity, courage and freedom from error in his own life to take right action. He was "guilty" of the same abuse.

This highly self-protective and self-interested stance may seem insignificant, but it is emblematic of a world-wide epidemic: the Code of Silence. It is the code of the ego and therefore the code of fear. It infiltrates each one of us on a personal level that jumps to local, national and global levels because the ego exists in everyone. Instead of helping others by correcting ourselves, we become witnesses or complicit participants and partners in the problems, which *compounds* by ten the negative karma of the world—and our own.

The only way to stop this pattern is to deal with our own negative karma. If Monty, for example, had examined himself, realized he was doing the same thing as the managers and then self-corrected, he would have been 'clean' in his own mind and nothing could have prevented him from telling the owners. Others would have admired his courage, gained the strength from it to correct themselves and joined together to present a united voice to the owners that could not have been ignored. If we all acted in the same manner, nothing could prevent us from taking corrective action in our own lives and then uniting to combat evil and error in the world.

Those of us unwilling to purge ourselves, however, prevent the universal expression of light, goodness, neutrality and peace, steering humanity's once sacred steps toward God into a mass march toward oblivion. But it needn't stay this way and, with Divine Mother close at hand, it won't.

Karma Defined

Karma means *cause and effect*. For each thought, word or deed (cause), there is an equal consequence (effect). There are two kinds of causes we can make: positive or negative. A positive cause produces a positive effect; a negative cause produces a negative effect.

A positive cause is a response. The word response comes from the French word *repondre*: to answer. A positive cause answers a situation, condition or person appropriately. If the positive cause of a response is made, the effect will be positive, and the situation, condition or person will be answered in healing harmony for all concerned.

A negative cause is a reaction. Reaction is a word literally meaning "to act again"—as in the unenlightened ways that did not work before; if they had worked, the situation, condition or person would not be in our lives. If the negative cause of a reaction is made, then the effect will be negative, and the situation, condition or person will persist.

If the negative cause remains uncorrected, then intensified consequences will be met at a subsequent point in time. This must occur, not only due to the "ten times law," but because we will continue to make mistakes based on the *original* negative cause. We will have to face the music at some point in regard to these additional mistakes, too.

Cause and effect, however, is not only karma; it is

creation. We are the creators of every cause we make, as well as each effect attributable to that cause. In addition, we are held accountable for both the cause and its effects. There is no getting out of this. It is how the universe works. It is how we were made by *our* Creators.

Even though karma is in constant, creative motion, the West has not been well-educated about it, so let's correct *that* error by looking now at a few examples of cause and effect. To make certain they are clear, most of the examples are dramatic, and there is a particular emphasis on <u>negative karma</u>. After all, anyone can tell us that doing good creates more good in our lives; it's understanding the bad so we can stop it that has become so troublesome.

> 1) You forgot to put the chicken in the refrigerator overnight. You ate it the next day and became violently ill.
> 2) When you were young, you tapped your brother on the head with a Tinker Toy. He slammed you back with a Tonka Truck.

Those are examples from which we learned quickly. Experiencing the negative effect of a negative cause just one time is enough to keep us from doing it again. Conversely, that is true in a positive context:

> 3) You were thirsty. You drank a glass of water and the thirst was quenched.
> 4) You found a purse and returned it. The grateful owner gave you a reward.

Ok. These make sense, but there is a point where karma gets really tricky. It is much harder to understand and much easier to dismiss karma altogether when:

> 5) You lied to your friend and told him that you weren't sleeping with his wife. He be-

lieved you—and nothing happened.

6) You absconded with millions from the company and retired to Bermuda. A rich aunt died and left you millions *more.*

7) You killed someone, but an innocent person was arrested. They went to jail and you went free.

The equally unexpected can happen when we are circumspect about doing only good in the world:

8) You gave your last dollar to a homeless person. The next month you lost your job, then your home, and had to seek shelter in a puptent.

9) You rescued a child from a burning building. Later an arsonist burned down your house and you noted on the way to the hospital, "'No good deed goes unpunished.'"

10) You led an admirable life. When a big earthquake hit, it spared every house but yours. You cried, "Why ME?"

11) You always honored your parents. Both were killed in a plane crash.

These things are not supposed to happen. There is an immaculate justice system inherent in the world to prevent such inequities from occurring—isn't there? God and the universe know better than to allow injustice. They are, after all, the creators of truth *and* justice—aren't they?

Yes. And this is how it works:

Every cause has a simultaneous effect. The simultaneity of cause and effect *ensures* the fact that truth and justice are in constant operation: no cause is executed without its effect in hand, and no effect is experienced without a cause.

We rely so heavily on our physical senses, however, that we are not always able to *see* the intrinsic simultaneity, at least not right away. We don't, for example, instantly see the simultaneity when it is applied to the question, "Which came first, the chicken or the egg?" The truth is that neither one came first; they came together: the chicken contains the egg, and the egg contains the chicken. But it takes time for an egg to develop into a chicken, just as it takes time for a chicken to lay an egg, before we can see that this is true.

And time is the key. Not only does it take time to understand that cause and effect, like truth and justice, always occur, but it is because of time that we lost the awareness in the first place.

Encountering Karma In Time

Just as God and the universe are the creators of truth and justice, we are the creators of time. The original version of Genesis 1:1 on page 151 notes we mistakenly decided free will means we are independent and separate from God; that one misperception gave birth to many others, including the illusion of time to replace the Reality of eternity.

Because we exist in the illusion of time, any cause we make is also executed in time. Its effect simultaneously occurs, but in the midst of all our other illusions. Since separation is one of the illusions, it will *seem*—like drizzling oil onto water in a bowl and then watching the droplets float away from each other—that the effect separated from its cause. In truth, the effect has just floated from, but is still connected to, its original cause.

What this means is that while there is an immediate effect for every cause, it will not be immediately *experienced*. Rather, like a droplet of oil floating to another point in the bowl, the effect drifts to *another point in time*—tomorrow, next week, next year or next lifetime. Because that is true, the effect may even *seem* to disappear and we may falsely believe there will never be a consequence. Worse, if a negative effect is experienced so far along the continuum of time that remembering the cause is impossible, we will never be able to make the connection and correct it.

As a different analogy, cause and effect in time can be likened to our emptying a bucket of trout in a pond. Even if we jump in for a swim, we will not necessarily see a fish right away. The more we stir up the water, clouding it with mud from the bottom of the pond, the less likely we will notice any fish at all—but sooner or later we will run into every last one of them. If we are floating on our back, soaking up the sunlight, a trout breaking through the water and nipping at our nose is not going to be perceived as an act of nature, but as a real surprise: "Where did *that* come from!"

Not bumping into one of the trout earlier, or not seeing one from the shore, plays into our great ability to deny. We forget the fish are there, never mind that we personally placed them in the pond. Instead of recognizing the fish as something we introduced earlier, we wonder what on earth they are doing in *our* pond—exactly the way we wonder why anything unanticipated suddenly surfaces in our lives.

Another example of not recognizing cause and effect is demonstrated by my dog, Ruby Keeler, so named because she loves to dance and then keel over. She will dance about the living room with a ball, nudge it quite a distance with her paw, and then be visibly shocked when the ball, hitting a chair, bounces back at her. She jumps away, alarmed and on the ready, viewing the chair as the mischievous cause, as if it had a life of its own and had bounced the ball back to her of its own accord. The chair is now untrustworthy; an otherwise static and inanimate object suddenly has power, and Ruby has no recognition of her own part in the drama.

My cat, Sophie, on the other hand, spent the first year of her life exploring the cause and effect of *everything*. No bug went unturned, no trellis unclimbed, no toilet unflushed without her little paws having a hand in figuring out how it worked. As a result, she has earned the right to sleep away the next ten years of her life in the total confidence that she has mastered this thing called cause and effect, while Ruby will be avoiding every chair on the planet until the end of time.

We could all be like Sophie, but we are all so much more like Ruby. We nudge the ball (make a cause) and see it come back (the effect) as if from the blue, not from ourselves. We do it again and again with the same results and lose faith in God and the universe when nothing changes. To stop making the same mistake, we need to go back to the first time we did it; we need to go back to the *original* cause of whatever is undesirable in our lives and correct it.

The Original Cause of Negative Karma

The importance of locating the original cause cannot be overstated; our freedom literally depends on it.

A Course in Miracles says that, "Your part is merely to return your thinking to the point at which the error was made." No time frame is delineated, however, which means the specific point may exist as far back as a past life. As Dr. Brian Weiss, the author of the acclaimed book, *Many Lives, Many Masters*, and others including myself now can attest, that is <u>exactly</u> where the point lies.

But trying to locate it ourselves can be like looking in our murky pond for the one trout that spawned all the rest. That is why ending negative karma has always been troublesome—it appears in the present as a problem, but when we realize we're in deep water because of it, its original cause is virtually impossible to find.

To complicate matters further, karma can be experienced tit for tat or an eye for an eye—but not always. Since the original cause was made in the illusion of time, its effect can spring up in a variety of forms not immediately attributable to *any* equivalent past action. For example, let's say that we raped a woman in a past life. In our current life we may not be raped in what would be the conventional act of retributive justice, but instead our mother, daughter, or sister is raped (as part of her negative karma). We were born into this particular family to understand first-hand the suffering our prior, identical act caused *others*; but while we experience the pain of the assault on a loved one, we can't connect it in any way to ourselves. This gives way to seemingly unanswerable questions, "Why me? Why my family? We never hurt anyone."

Worse, however, and the kicker in terms of complications, is that the same scenario can occur even if we did not rape anyone, but participated by goading someone to rape, witnessing a rape without attempting to stop it, or becoming aware of the rapist and not reporting them.

In short, then, negative karma can be experienced:

1) in different guises
2) through various sources
3) from diverse causes
4) *and* in current or future time

All of these contributing components can create a conundrum out of what was, once, a simple original cause. The next section, however, sheds enough light on karma to make its original cause exceptionally easy to identify and then dissolve. If you are thinking, "Oh, thank God!" you are right, but we will get to Her in a minute.

How Karma Works

Time is not linear. Time is actually far more like that pond with the trout. It is easier, however, for the rational part of our minds to understand just now in a linear way. For that reason, then, let's take a look at a linear time-line to see how karma works. Each ^ represents a particular cause repeated or intensified over time, and each * represents the dispersed and therefore future effect.

```
------- ^ ------ ^ -------- ^ ^ ^ ---- -- ^ --------------------******--
  1500    1600     1700      1800      1900        2020
```

For the sake of example, let's say the particular cause being represented is murder. In the 1500's we are part of a work-team building a cathedral in France. The architect is worried about how we positioned a spire, but we misinterpret his concern as a personal criticism, a theft of honor. An argument ensues; we hit him, he fires us. We were in error, but in our minds a theft of honor escalated into the theft of our livelihood; we blame the architect and the anger is never resolved. In the 1600's we hit a co-worker in England; it felt so good, we celebrate with a pint at the pub. Another altercation occurs in the 1700's in Wales. Our pay is stolen; we know the thief is the man we just fought with. Unable to prove it, we are so angry we plan his murder. He hears of our intent and moves to America; we follow, but never find him. The energy against him is not resolved and results in our accidentally killing a vagrant when he tries to pick our pocket. No witnesses, no consequences; we rationalize our action as what thieves deserve. In the 1800's we are helping build the transcontinental railroad through the Sierra Nevada Mountains. "Coolies" are hired on as cheap labor and in our minds steal from us a good living. A brawl breaks out; we take advantage of it and deliberatelly kill the foreman who hired the Chinese laborers. His death is ruled accidental.

In the 1900's the violence stops. Perhaps this is due to unacknowledged guilt from the past that we confuse with fear of reprisal from the mob as we now build up a successful restaurant business in New York. If not, the threat from the mob might be enough to stop anyone for a time; or, the conditions in the 1900's are not sufficiently irritating to evoke what has become the full-blown reaction of murder to injustice. We don't commit murder this life-time, but neither do we consciously self-correct the habituated tendency toward it. The effects from the past therefore continue to be projected into future time. As a result, we are murdered in cold blood at work in the year 2020. Folks grieve, "How could this happen to such a nice person!" and bemoan the injustice of our death without understanding that justice has just been perfectly served.

This is very difficult to accept when one looks only at

the nice person slaughtered at work without reviewing their past-life history. It makes us want to think they were simply in the wrong place at the wrong time. Even if that were true, and let's say for the sake of argument it is, we still need to ask, "How is it they were *in* the wrong place? What mistakes were made in judgment to lead them physically to this moment and this particular consequence?"

No one deserves to be murdered, nor does anyone deserve to become a murderer. In either case, however, whether it seems so or not, the negative karma *is there*, and it is saying that if the person had been given in their past lives the love and compassion we feel for them now, from themselves or from others, they never would have made the causes creating such a disastrous effect.

This is so true that when anyone's negative karma is similarly viewed, it is impossible not to feel *tremendous* sympathy, "Oh, no. If they had been given the love they needed to correct a misperception long ago, this wouldn't have happened." In addition, since love prohibits error from being made in *any* given moment, the misperception itself would not have happened. These are very important reasons why Christ asks us to love one another. But an additional reason He asks, one often overlooked, is for our *own* salvation:

Every positive response or negative reaction we have toward another person is a karmic cause *in our own lives*. It will be returned to us as part of the mirroring consequence of karma noted in the chapter entitled *Knowing*, ensuring a first-hand understanding of the effects of all of our actions, words and thoughts. Because feelings come from thoughts, they are equal creators of karma; our feelings must be loving or those returned to us will be loveless, too. Every negative emotion, then, must be transcended with love and compassion for our *own* sake, as well as for the other person, and it can be. When we encounter or hear of someone in distress, experiencing severe problems or doing terrible things, instead of judging them, we can consider the fact, for their sake *and* ours, that the only thing really going on is the unresolved karma in their life based on one uncorrected misperception, an original error, long ago. Giving them love now will help heal that misperception and help guarantee our own karmic protection from lovelessness in the future.

A positive response may mean leaving a negative or hurtful person, but we must still maintain love, compassion and gratitude for them, and we can. The deluded can evoke gratitude that we are sane; the destructive that we are constructive; the miserable that we are joyous; the brutal that we are kind, and so on. As this recognition takes place, we experience intensified value of ourselves, and realize by the contrast how hard it must be to be the other person. This brings compassion for them and coupled with compassion is love. Just feeling these emotions sends them out to be telepathically received by that person, literally supporting them in their need. By the law of cause and effect, the support is then returned to *us* from someone else; that person in turn is supported by another, and so it continues as one after another is blessed by our initial gratitude for one person.

The time-line on page 191 can be used for any negative karma, so let's say as another example that we need support standing up for ourselves. In the 1500's we have a falling-out with a fellow weaver in the Norwich guildhall who doesn't like our quilt pattern; deeply hurt, we say nothing. In the early 1600's a courtier, jealous of our close relationship with the Queen as Her seamstress, convinces the aging Elizabeth our designs make her look old, but we do nothing to protect our reputation; when asked to leave the Court, we do. By the 1700's we have no confidence in our work and agree it is better to stay home and knit sweaters for the little ones. In the 1800's we avoid the issue by traveling to London once a year to buy the family's clothes. In the 1900's we sit by the fire—and watch it. In the year 2020 we commit suicide because we believe we have no viable talent.

Again, should love have entered at any prior point in time—from those observing the situation, those provoking it, or from the individual involved—no one would be taking their life now. Love would have been the preventive of pain, the healing of low self-esteem, and the immunity against either one ever beginning.

It is calculated in Buddhism that we have the opportunity to select from among 3,000 responses or reactions in a given moment. Each decision in thought, word, deed or feeling carries *some* weight. Over time, all of these causes create a tendency in a certain area, making karma *the tendency toward the repeated selection of the same thought, word, deed or feeling no matter how many choices are offered in a given moment.* We become so entrenched in our particular pattern of cause and effect, so habituated to specific reactions, that at some point we may not even realize other choices exist.

It is easy to see from the two past-life examples that while we think for a number of centuries there are no consequences to a particular action or attitude, a sorry surprise is in store for us. Yet, that is how the scales of justice are really weighed. Too many *** in one area without correction and the scales tip to one side, the universe goes into overload, and negative karmic consequence—*the accumulated effects of a repeatedly uncorrected cause*—is activated at the precise point in time at which the scales tip.

Justice is so immaculate, so precise, and so particular to the individual, no one should ever ask, "Why *me*?" and without waiting for an answer, add the disaster to a growing list of God's misdemeanors against us. Instead, the question should be sincerely posed, "Why *did* this happen to me?" and then ask Divine Mother for the answer, because there is one and She knows what it is.

We will be pursuing that later in detail, but a related reason to go to Divine Mother is that *no one has the karma to suffer. No one.* Suffering should be experienced as an alarm in our lives, not a snooze button; it is going off to awaken us to the light and truth that the karmic situation brings with it. At the first sound of the alarm, the first hint of suffering, we should never go back to sleep, but get up and immediately ask Divine Mother what is really going on, why it is going on, how to see it correctly and exactly what to do about it, because She will tell us and, in the telling, awaken us to a new life of calm, happiness and peace.

While we will pursue this in detail, too, it should be noted now that there is always a wonderful surprise in karma—but we won't know what it is if we don't ask. For example, I thought I did something awful to merit my father as a parent, but it was the opposite: in 18th-century Chantilly, France, he was violent toward my 16-year-old daughter. It was my desire, out of enormous compassion for him, to have him as a father at the same age this lifetime in order to offer him another chance—the chance to choose love and light.

It is greatly to our benefit, then, to seek the past-life reasons for certain situations in order to release ourselves from guilt or anger in the present, and realize how good we really are. If this isn't done, if we don't know why something is happening in our lives whether we have directly caused it or not, our actions will be in error; they will compound the karma instead of heal it, and the karma will return until we do—just as the following demonstrates.

A Second Look

Let's go back to the examples on pages 186-187.

5) Adultery:

Even though nothing happens in this lifetime, it does not mean you have gotten away with anything. You can be assured that justice will appear in a later life and, when you discover then that your wife is having an affair with one of your friends, you will either go mad with jealousy, having denied the initial cause from the lifetime in question—or you will take a moment to remember the truth: your chickens have simply come home to roost.

6) Embezzlement:

While it seems embezzlement was being rewarded with an inheritance, it wasn't at all. One doesn't have anything to do with the other. The inheritance came from good deeds in the distant past, while the effect from the cause of embezzlement will materialize in a future life—perhaps the company you have worked long and hard to establish will be wiped out overnight in a stock market crash or devoured by a hostile take-over. Whatever the case may be, you will demand "Why *me!*" or you'll be smarter—you will realize there must have been a previous cause, make the determination to find out what it was, and then correct it. Once the connection and correction are made, the pain, guilt, blame and attack cease, and the opportunity to rebuild in legitimate ways presents itself.

7) Murder:

This scenario is one of the ego's favorites because it is the epitome of injustice: you got away with murder while someone else took the rap. In a future lifetime, however, you will be the one behind bars for a murder you didn't commit, screaming "I didn't do it!"—and you didn't, not in this lifetime, but certainly in the other. The amount of time it takes to free you in the future life will be the just amount of time you should have served in the prior one.

8) Homelessness:

This one is pitiful. There you were, trying to do the right thing, and what did you get for it? A puptent. This exemplifies too little too late, because any dollar from you, first or last, will not pay the debt acquired during a previous lifetime in the 11th century, say, in which you were a soldier and swept down on some unsuspecting town, confiscating for the king every home in sight down to the last hut.

Karma does not necessarily involve the same person or persons. It can go on quite well about its business without the original cast of characters, although a memorable face or two may be in sight. If the homeless person, for example, was one of the unsuspecting souls in a hut, chances are he wasn't thrilled with just a dollar.

9) Arson:

This could be a continuation of #8. If you didn't want the houses for the king, but didn't want them for the people either, you may have just burned them down, the inhabitants along with them. Or it could be that you burned Atlanta during the Civil War and killed your own cousins, or perhaps there was an addiction to arson in 17th-century England by which you delighted in setting fire to an inviting thatched roof and the whole village went up. When a serious lack of personal responsibility killed a multitude, saving one life won't cut the karma, but discovering a vaccine that enables many to live, for instance, would certainly send the scales of justice tipping in the right direction.

The comment "No good deed goes unpunished," is worth exploration. It is a remark that, like so many others, is not meant seriously—but it is unconsciously heard very seriously, and it connects the effect to the wrong cause; in this particular example, we can come to believe that punishment is inevitable no matter what we do. If the ego loved #8, it is ecstatic about this one because it promotes the attitude that morality doesn't pay, which in turn guarantees future lives filled with karmic consequences of this very error. When an amoral soul returns to the earth plane, *and it will*, there will be only more of the same, because we are required to encounter our own creations here so that we may correct them. *For our own sake as creators,* we are not allowed to avoid learning cause and effect.

An example of this return is the number of younger and younger children committing heinous crimes. The soul committing them earlier in time never confronted the error and never corrected. It has returned in criminal motion to the very environment and genetic make-up conducive to the perpetuation of that motion. The death of the person will not stop the proclivity to criminal action any more than capital punishment will stop forever the person who has committed a capital crime. Death kills the body, not the ego, and the ego will return hand in hand with the soul, in another body, to *be* corrected. Unless the person is restored to truth and consciously corrected, they will return to kill and be killed by virtue of the karmic law of cause and effect.

10) <u>Earthquake:</u>

You can lose your house to an earthquake or other natural disaster for any number of past, or past-life, reasons, all of them karmically sound: having been a bank manager and deprived a qualified applicant a house loan due to the color of their skin; having found a way to deny the inheritance of a house to the rightful heir, whether you gained financially from it or not; killing a mother or father and depriving a child of the security of a family, which a home *represents*; not regarding ownership of a home with gratitude, but as a right; being envious of a landowner and his or her property; not having stood up against evil when the opportunity was presented, thereby causing another to lose faith in God and the universe, when God and the universe are the only security and real home anyone has ... and so on.

11) <u>Parent's Death:</u>

This one is easy. How many parents did you kill without a second thought in numbers 8, 9 and 10?

Any of us might ask, "Why me?" in a particular situation, but an observer in possession of all the facts, past and present, would ask, "Why *not* you?" We just have not lived long enough with seeing eyes to be able to view the past projected into the future, when the future really is just today—delayed.

When it comes to questions like these, most of us do not phrase them correctly. If you are disfigured in a car accident, for example, the question is not whether the driver of the other car can be sued, but "Whom did I deface in the past?" by slandering them. Similarly, if you are run over by a train, the question is not only why didn't the guardrail come down, but "Whom did I once railroad?" If you are not finding true love and wonder where it is, the right question is, "How can I be truly loveable?" If the perfect mate has not been found, ask "Perfect for what?" Every person is perfect for a lesson that, once learned, *will* attract naturally the desired alliance.

There are some phrases in common usage, such as,

"Oh, life dealt him a bad hand," and "Play the cards God gave you." These are misnomers and add to mounting world misinformation, because the cards life dealt us, or the cards we think God gave us, were first selected personally *by us*. Nothing is taken from us that we did not covet or in some way fail to value before, just as nothing is denied that we did not deny another or ourselves first. Conversely, no one receives an abundance that was not in some way once earned, just as no one gathers acclaim that is not in some way deserved. No one is given good fortune without having made the causes in the past to justify it in the present—which can be as simple as not obstructing the flow of God's good with their own negative karma in that particular area.

Not remembering these things leads us to make long-term judgements about the world and the people in it that are not sound, and that is where the ego thinks it has us. As long as karma comes out of left field, with the appearance of injustice, and without an easily traceable cause, we will *never* be free of it. Yet, we *can* end negative karma, end it easily, and end it without multiple lifetimes to do it, just by shifting from the problem to the Source of the solution; to the One who rectifies all error by knowing the original cause of the negative karma; to She who can properly phrase questions before answering them for us: the Heart of the correcting sphere of light and love, Divine Mother God.

The world can seem brutally cruel if we don't understand that only our negative karma is the problem and that Divine Mother is here to solve it, even if Her presence isn't real to us. The *Lotus Sutra* says that when we don't value the Buddha, we don't desire him and he disappears; that causes us to realize his value, which increases the desire for him and so he returns. Divine Mother, the Mother of the Buddhas, comes and goes for the same reasons and in the same manner, waxing and waning like the moon with which She is associated for its similar action.

But in truth the Buddha only *appears* to come and go. The moon only *appears* to wax and wane—how much we see of it depends on how much sunlight is directd to it. It is the same with Divine Mother. When we realize She has value, we let our desire for Her direct our light to Her, and She returns to conscious focus. We see then how close She has always been, how ready She is to reveal the original cause of our negative karma—and how just revealing it will heal it.

Spiritual healing isn't like finding a tear in the soul and mending it. It is the conscious recognition of our perfect wholeness no matter what was done to us or what we have done. And that recognition is exactly what occurs when Divine Mother enables us to experience the truth that comes so conveniently attached to the original error: *even the worst things we have done are completely retractable in the light.*

She makes certain we understand how this can be: our mistakes were made *only* in the illusion of time, which means on a spiritual level—the only level that truly exists—they aren't real; they too are only illusion, and that is why they are no more permanent than a pencil mark. No matter how bad they seem, they can be entirely erased in the light of this understanding, as can every one of their effects, and we needn't go further than our own mind to do it.

We just meet Divine Mother in Divine Meditation and participate with Her in the enlightening, exhilarating and liberating experience called the Spiritual Process. For this She has waited. For this She is here. For this, turn the page.

18

The Spiritual Process

Because the Spiritual Process is not common knowledge, most people don't know to try it. Even if they did, who among us wants to stop in the middle of a busy schedule to meditate and look at what we did in the past? Avoiding that kind of guilt is why we *have* a busy schedule.

When Ty was a baby, guilt began for me the instant I was semi-conscious in the morning. Like many of us, I felt so helplessly at fault for things in the past which could not be changed that I would jump up to get away from the memories and plunge into activity until night removed the day—but not the guilt. I would awaken in the middle of the night and find myself already running from the bedroom to the front door for escape, my heart pounding, as unaddressed issues pursued me like a lynch mob for the hanging.

That was my reaction to the sins of the past before realizing they are erasable error, and before Divine Mother showed me how to look at guilt: while it seems that guilt is a reminder of the bad things we have done and we therefore are bad, it is actually, paradoxically, telling us we are good and not to feel guilty. If we lied to a friend, for example, we feel guilt because we are *not* liars; we are innately honest but failed to remember it or act on it in that moment. To believe otherwise is to betray our own integrity—which couldn't be betrayed if it were not there. All goodness is there. So while guilt seems to condemn who we are, we can use it to look at who we *really* are. It is important to thank the guilt for alerting us to the truth of our goodness; savor the goodness, and privately thank everyone involved in each episode of guilt; playing their part gave us the opportunity to validate our true identity. Once guilt is acknowledged this way—"I'm so good, that's why I was feeling so bad!"—it *leaves*.

If we can't see the truth, Divine Mother can. Leslie, a sweet, 20-year-old friend who is very interested in Divine Mother, enthusiastically wondered not long ago, "What did She *say*?" about this and that. Leslie so sincerely wanted to know more that I sent her the first Divine Meditation tape in a series created by Divine Mother to bring us all back to the light—but oddly there was no response. When I spoke with Leslie again and asked if she had listened to the tape, she whispered, "I can't. I don't want to know."

That wasn't the truth, and then it dawned on me, "Are you scared because of the abortion you had?" She answered, "Yes. God will punish me."

I know Divine Mother's arms would open in Divine Meditation at the speed of light to embrace the child hurt by the abortion: the one talking to me on the other end of the line. I told Leslie this, and that if the abortion—or any other action in her life—had been a mistake, Divine Mother would explain how it could be resolved now. She would also supply the past-life reasons for this or any circumstance in her or the father's life. If the abortion were not in error, then Divine Mother would say so, adding that the incoming soul was highly aware of its loving and unselfish purpose in this context; since we don't always enter the body at conception, it is very possible that no soul's journey was interrupted.

Whenever we are confronted by a difficult decision, Divine Mother says, "The real issue is whether the decision will be made in the light." The best of all outcomes, then, would have been Leslie asking Divine Mother for guidance *before* any action was taken so that she could have been told the purpose of the pregnancy. How the child was conceived and *perceived* are such critical aspects, too, that, were it necessary, Divine Mother would have kindly corrected Leslie's perception of the baby, sex and conception, and then told her the best choice to be made and *why it would be best*.

There are so many karmic variables for each individual, it is impossible to make a truly informed decision without the knowledge of Divine Mother. In addition, fear and anxiety alter perception to such a degree in a crisis that the event can seem overwhelming when it really is not. It is *very* important, then, to practice Divine Meditation in advance of needing it, because without prior experiences of hurdling over everyday fear and anxiety to reach the truth in meditation, it can seem as overwhelming as the crisis, and this very real way out of it will be avoided entirely.

That said, it is never too late to bring an issue to Divine Mother. In Leslie's case, asking Her for help *at any point in time* would have, as it still would, release her from the constricting fear of guilt. It would, in fact, pull down this invisible barrier erected between her negative assessment of the abortion and the liberating truth about herself within.

But Leslie's decision not to ask at all, based on a false assumption, a misperception, creates more error. Any move away from the truth is a move away from her own enlightenment, as it is for any of us who resist the light. Guilt must be resolved, or mistaken action will be taken in reaction to *it*, never mind in reaction to what caused it. Compounding the problem this way removes her further from Divine Mother, who is only asking, as She asks all of us, "For your own sake, sweetheart, don't you want to see this as it truly is?"

The Importance of Personal Retrieval

I could have obtained the information for Leslie, but no one has the right to eclipse another person's opportunity to experience knowledge directly. As helpful as psychics can be by reading past lives or giving direction in this one, they provide a serious disservice as well. They generally do not teach others that this ability is in us all; nor do they offer the ways to access it, and then rely on encouragement, patience, faith and prayer to turn the person toward the light on their own. Instead, psychics give the impression that being able to access truth is a rare gift.

It isn't rare. Rather, how to access it correctly is rarely revealed and the benefits to the individual rarely explained. If they were, this would be an enlightened planet.

The recounting of a past life by someone else is also a serious disservice for another reason. It deprives the recipient of their own emotional and pictorial history. Going to a psychic is like sending someone else to Disneyland and believing their report is our experience, their photographs our memory. That is not real or true and therefore not meaningful, when past lives we personally access are a consistent source of highly impacting, enlightening and truthful information.

Once, Pia did a past life reading for me. It was possible to follow along, observing the scenes in my mind, but I was too removed to relive them. That lifetime in Spain held the seeds of a tendency toward an early death and a sincere quest for spirituality, but it never had the emotional energy or connection to truth for me as did the lives I was able to access in Divine Meditation and *re-experience* with Divine Mother. Since this one was retrieved by Pia, I did not experience the numinosity that is *mandatory* for understanding, transformation and healing. As mentioned before, healing is not ever like finding a tear in the soul and mending it. It is realizing that our true identity is forever whole and intact *despite* the slings and arrows which have come our way. That realization can only occur in direct relationship with the images of the past life itself, and as Divine Mother presents and explains them.

There is additional significance to personal retrieval. Information from a past life brought internally to one's own awareness is so vibrant, vital and valid that it cannot be denied; it connects with inner awareness and we *know* it is true. At the same time, the inherent lessons come to consciousness with such clarity and force that they can't be ignored. In contrast, a past life is easy to deny and ignore when someone else seems to be spinning a tale out of the blue and putting our name on it.

In 1985, four years after re-meeting Divine Mother, I went to a good psychic. He said many things, among them that a woman on the other side, who had been like a mother to me since childhood, was guiding and protecting me now. I went home and immediately called the mother of a childhood friend who *had* been like a mother to me, wondering if she had passed over. Since Edna answered the phone, she was not the mystery woman. I later realized, of course, that it was Divine Mother. If you compare the psychic's accurate reading, but misleading interpretation, with the impact actually knowing Divine Mother has made on me and my life, you can see *there is no comparison.*

By not being informed of the real advantages of personal retrieval, we put it off, losing the opportunity to heal and to receive some of the most important information that can be found within, the very crux of the Spiritual Process itself: God's will in our lives.

God's Will

There are three wills vying for attention in our mind: God's will, the ego's will, and free will.

Free will offers us the choice of following God's will or the ego's will—which, when all is said and done, is effectively no choice at all. That is because the ego would be very happy to see our body confined to a coffin somewhere, the soul forever hanging about it in a futile effort to get back in, while God's will offers everlasting freedom in the here and now—body or not. As hard as it may be to accept at first, free will is an illusion fabricated by the ego, because after understanding what it really wants for us, we will know the only will that can *ever* provide real happiness is God's.

In truth, the will of the Mother and Father *is* free will, but in the sense of wanting *our will free from the ego* so we can come Home again, a freedom that naturally occurs when we realize our true identity as a child of God. To that end, we only have to follow the Biblical advice, "Knock and it shall be opened to you," which is to say, knock at the door of Divine Meditation, it opens, and we are Home again. That is when we know who we are, that we are more than wanted by God and, because we are wanted, we will make the adjustments necessary to stay Home in our minds and in our lives while here on earth.

This isn't difficult, but going into Divine Meditation requires our willingness to step past the ego's *unwillingness*. The ego is adamant we never see all the illusions it has meticulously placed over God's loving will since the beginning of time. For example, the ego has always warned that God's will is not only judgmental and never in our favor, but a pandora's box we should dread opening because inside is a list of unsavory tasks ahead, not to mention an itemized bill for "Services Rendered." Once these accounts are settled, there is another surprise: a bundle of home videos capturing every second of this lifetime in excruciating detail.

Surreptitiously recorded under the sadistic auspices of some celestial version of "Smile! You're on Candid Camera!" these videos will be run on the inner screen of our mind in meditation so that we can be reminded of our failures and experience the humiliation all over again. Further, the tapes will be run in slow motion just in case we did not feel bad the first time and, if that weren't enough, the pause button will function automatically for all those times we didn't even know we did anything wrong.

That is just in life. Death is an eternal re-run.

Since this has proven sufficient to keep us from meditation, Divine or otherwise, let's get straight on God's will by backing up a second to discover how it was we got so sidetracked by the ego as to believe condemnation inevitable.

Denial

Since we have free will, we may meet any situation with either a response or a reaction. Response is of God (in the light), while reaction is of the ego (out of the light). Response always reveals God's will in our lives, while reaction—like Leslie's guilt, for example—conceals it.

The ego loves reaction because it is always wrong. In addition, doing or thinking the wrong thing builds up stress, leads to cancer, heart attack or stroke, *and* keeps us locked in illusions. So, how has the ego managed to keep us reacting instead of responding? Like this:

We cannot escape our problems until we escape the illusions that created them, but we cannot escape the illusions until we find the right response. We cannot find the right response until we meditate, but we cannot meditate because we need the ego's cooperation to do it. We cannot *get* the ego's cooperation to meditate because it will not give any, so we are never able to find the right response, leaving us no choice *but* reaction. Reaction then creates more problems which cannot be solved with the right response, so we are back where we started, only with a new host of misadventures to add to the list, dooming us forever, and that, frankly, is enough to give anyone a heart attack.

To perpetuate this negative cycle, the ego generally stands somewhere in the dark shadows of our mind, advising, "Don't listen to Divine Mother. Do whatever you want and pretend you never did it, thought it or said it. No one will ever know." This should be heard as "No one will ever know—*not even you*," because the ego is proposing the perfect way to prevent reconciliation with the truth: denial. Looking for the easy way out, and rarely reckoning the cost, denial seems like a good option. We do not want to think about things or really look at them, so we don't.

Divine Mother, however, is well aware of our denial and cannot allow us to forget—not as a means of punishment, but to protect our light from all those sticky-backed illusions of the ego that will in time shut our eyes and mind with the glue of guilt. She will, therefore, always remind us:

1) The problem is the ego's *misperception* of Reality. Our denial just keeps us from realizing this is true.

2) We need to bring the misperception to Her. She will reveal it as a mistake and why it is one. Truth will then take its place, the problem will dissolve, and we will be free.

3) Exposure to Her light *always* transforms the negative of a problem into a color photograph of our beauty as a child of God.

The way to do all of this successfully opens up when we are willing to refuse denial long enough to meditate instead. Divine Mother will then carry us the rest of the way, right into the freedom of the Spiritual Process with Her.

The Spiritual Process

First, everything in our life or a past life *is* recorded, not on video, but on the skein of time and space. It is an ethereal library of our every feeling, thought, word and deed as it occurred. If we would remember that the ill-chosen ones are recorded as vividly as the Rodney King beating, only 24 hours a day for each one of us, we wouldn't do anything wrong. But we do forget, and what we have particularly forgotten is the original error that created whatever negative karma we are experiencing in the present. The grace of Divine Mother, however, allows us to remember.

This is how that grace works and why:

By Divine Design, *the original error (the original cause)* from a past life is removed from the skein of time and space, and placed in our lives as a problem *(the effect)*. The problem is played out in specific life-situations, dreams, Divine Meditation and/or all three, giving us the opportunity to use our "free" will to undo the error by handling it correctly this time. We can choose the ego's will and react (deny the solution and guarantee the problem's later return at ten times the intensity), *or* we can choose God's will and respond by talking to Divine Mother and asking Her how to resolve the problem forever.

If we choose God's will, we learn directly from Divine Mother's words, images and transforming numinosity that every problem was *always and only* created by a misperception of a situation, person, or ourselves. The misperception is corrected the instant She gives us the information needed to understand how it happened, and She will. Once understood, any error proceeding from the misperception—past, present or future—collapses, and truth takes its place. The problem now authentically resolved, it is removed from the skein of time and space as if it never happened, because on a spiritual level and in terms of Reality, it *didn't* happen; as a misperception, it was an illusion from start to finish. It only seemed real in our minds, and that is why it had to be returned to our minds for conscious resolution.

When a problem appears, then, it is only a Parental knock at *our* door, asking us to come Home this way: a) look at the problem's real cause; b) understand why it happened and self-forgiveness automatically follows; c) release it, the automatic result of forgiveness, and d) see the wonderful truth that remains—"For your own sake, sweetheart, don't you want to see this as it truly is?"

Divine Mother calls these steps the "Spiritual Process," and they are outlined in full below. Their value comes only from *experiencing* them, not from attaining a theoretical or intellectual understanding of them. When experienced, they are immediately effective *without fail* and bountiful as well, because removing the roadblocks to our good *always* allows our heart's desires to flow naturally into our lives.

THE SPIRITUAL PROCESS

1. Isolating the karmic problem
2. Locating the original cause
3. Explanation
4. Understanding

5. Realization of the illusion
6. Apology
7. Forgiveness
8. Release
9. Only truth remains

The best visual example of what the Spiritual Process pulls up in one fell swoop may be seen in this pictorial of a weed. It is a deceptively attractive plant, even flowering for us—which is exactly why we have let it flourish for so many lifetimes.

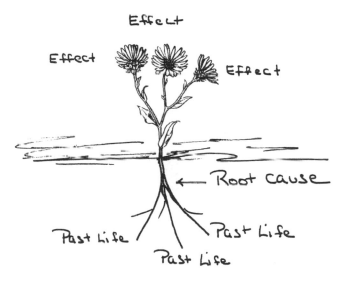

We can see the problem thriving vigorously above ground. Its flowering stems symbolize the various effects of that problem and show how they shut out any neighboring, healthy growth in the bargain. Below ground, deep in the unconscious, is a view we haven't seen since a seventh-grade science class when we had no idea such a boring sight would one day illustrate our salvation: the hardy main root representing the *root cause* of the weed's existence. This is the original cause, the original error. The smaller, off-shooting roots symbolize the past lives in which the original error was acted on. Not correcting the error contributed to the growth of the main root—and therefore to the continued existence of our weedy problem.

When we undertand it in this way, we will not want to keep any of it—and we won't have to. As you will see by example in the next chapter, exposure to the light and truth of Divine Mother kills the main root, making the Spiritual Process the crown of all processes: every emotional, psychological, mental and physical condition related to the root problem at any point in time—past, present or projected into the future—is pulled up as well, making room for healthy, life-sustaining, and abundant growth.

Not a trace of the negative karma remains in any area of our lives, and the energy once used to keep it in place is released and revitalized, made fresh and new for us, ready to be sent out by us, in any form, in any direction, for any higher purpose. As that energy flies out to embrace and encompass everything around it, we fly with it, higher and higher, too—all because we closed the lid on the Pandora's box of ego-guilt by opening the treasure chest of God's light.

Like the caterpillar slipping into the silky dark envelope of its cocoon, we entered into the soft darkness of the unconscious through Divine Meditation and followed Divine Mother's lantern to the truth. We were transformed by Her light in the Spiritual Process and emerged a butterfly, born anew. And now, because we finally know the truth as it really is, we can know the world as it really is: neutral, in harmony, and no matter what others project onto it, a place of peace.

19

The Spiritual Process
in Action

Some people who attend my lectures on Divine Mother are ready for the Spiritual Process. During a Guided Divine Meditation, they are returned to the original error by Divine Mother in less than 15 minutes, and the negative effects are removed. For others, a sustained period of preparation with Her is required to reach that point. Regardless of when it occurs, the Spiritual Process works the same way.

Because that is true, I would like to share my own experience with you and how any lingering effects of the people and situations you have read about in my life vanished. It was so stunning when it was done that, as unimaginable as it seems, I literally had to ask Divine Mother, "Did I *really* have any negative karma this lifetime?"

The period of preparation for me began a year before the near-death on Mother's Day, 1988. Crystal clean skies, soft breezes, fragrant shrubs, ancient trees, and mountains in exquisitely defined relief produced a glimpse of heaven only seen in California. After many years of unexplained silence on her part, and as many years of prayer on mine, my mother and I were finally speaking again. She still had problems, more severe than I realized, but it was wonderful to have a mom again. As I drove to visit her, Divine Mother suggested returning to the house in Arcadia where we had lived when she was ill. It was so important, I didn't ask why, but my mother was understandably reluctant. "Mom, I'll hold your hand, if you hold mine." She took a deep breath, put her hand in mine and agreed. We went, apprehensively expecting all the bad memories, but were astonished to find *none*. This was such a God-given altering of perception that she and I stepped into another dimension at the same time, asking, "Am I in a body or not?" "Am I—dead?" but we were led then to experience it, not question it.

The house was surrounded by glistening grass and sky-bound trees: periwinkle blue blossoms cascaded from the graceful limbs of jacarandas, others flowered in golden-pinks as if they had auras spun from the mid-spring sun, and a maple in fresh green leaf, scarcely once a sapling, stood its ground in front of my old bedroom, a giant. Memories tried to come forward then as I sat in the car with my mother and looked out, but ... where was it she had tried to drink herself to death? The windows of that room were now framed by curtains welcoming in the light. But wasn't that the camellia bush by the porch where I had cried after finding her suicide note—yet how could that be? There were only shiny emerald leaves and the flushed pink faces of the flowers bowing in the breeze. But the driveway where the paramedics had taken her away—no, it was lined with rose bushes, a butterfly gracing a perfect petal.

What did I think had been so horrible?

My mother and I, still holding hands, looked at each other in disbelief, and then stared out of the car again. It was too beautiful to speak. The past and its illusions of despair had never happened. There was only truth and light revealing the splendor of Reality. On this Mother's Day, Her day, Divine Mother was giving us a miracle.

Later that week, Divine Mother told me there would be greater enlightenment and truth than this. What I came to learn She meant is that the past had been removed here as an introduction to how it would be removed from consciousness by the near-death, and then removed from memory and the skein of time and space by the Spiritual Process. I did not, however, think the transformation of illusion into truth that day would continue only for me. My mother and I were very different, but the defining difference now was one of will: I would only go forward from this point on, and my mother would only go back. It was very painful to see. I kept hoping that since Reality can be chosen any time, my mother would choose it, too, but one night in 1990 Divine Mother presented a clairvoyant dream that would begin to awaken me from what I wanted to be true to what I had to face:

> My mother was late for a trolley. She ran down the steps of the station in her haste to catch it, reached for it, held on for a second and then fell off, tumbling down the remaining steps. I didn't know whether to scream for help or chant for her. I decided to chant and did. Her eyes fluttered open briefly and then closed. She wasn't going to live.

It was such a powerful nightmare I woke up screaming, and it upset me for weeks. The unconscious tugged at my mind; there was a vital nugget of information in a pun about the trolley. I couldn't "get" it, and then it surfaced as clear as a bell: "My mother is off her trolley."

That couldn't be—but she had reverted to so many of the old ways and already wasn't speaking to me again. I did not want to deal with such a sad circumstance, but I would be forced to by something related to the mother that came up next as a problem: the uterus. Fibroid tumors in the uterus had been a concern for a few years; I had even been admitted to Aspen Valley Hospital literally in grave condition the year before, hemorrhaging. They were suddenly so serious when she as suddenly stopped talking to me that an operation was required to remove them. It was *very* upsetting to know that while I had always been there for my mother, in spirit and in fact, she was not there, again, for me. I loved my mother, but I could no longer tolerate the repetitive negative karma with her that now boded *another* ten years of silence on her part. I turned to Divine Mother for the right response, and the karma would end then in the final transition from the mother on earth to the One always there for me. This conversation occurred on May 18, 1991:

Wendy: Please tell me what's going on.

Divine Mother: Nothing. You have tumors that will be removed. Don't worry. Your mother is cause here, not the misuse of creation. [I had wondered if the uterus symbolized the mother or creation.] You must forgive her fully, child. She is not in her/your right mind. You perceive her one way, she perceives herself another; both are incorrect—she is not as little as she sees herself, not as close to realizing potential as you hope. Please listen to Me. You're the mother here and always have been.

Wendy: (after a lifetime of concern over my mother) I hate thinking about this.

Divine Mother: (sweetly) Please listen to Me. You don't understand that she can't do it and will not this lifetime. Do not assume she can do anything because she can't. Relax in this and know you chose her for this very reason: to know Me. To know Mother Love that is real and true.

Wendy: Oh, that makes me very happy.

Divine Mother: There was another way, to lose her in death, but the wrong message would have been given to you about Me [that the Mother God could die away]. Use her to acknowledge your Self to the highest good for mankind. *Be* the Divine Mother she is not.

Wendy: Why do I feel I must help her?

Divine Mother: Because the ego would like you to spend your life fulfilling her nightmare of anxiety, tension and despair. That is her nightmare, hers alone. Please believe Me. She can't correct lifetimes of self-centeredness [but] you planted seeds of recovery for her.

Wendy: (sigh, very relieved to have her future recovery confirmed) Mother, why am I so pushed to complete this cycle?

Divine Mother: To complete this cycle is your destiny. Tumor is anger knot because of past influences lacking nurturing. You had many lifetimes without a mother, many lifetimes—*for your benefit*.

Wendy: This is so hard, not hard right now [nothing is hard in Divine Meditation. Then, as I "get" it:] Her ego is trying to keep my attention on her, like it always has, when the magnificence of the God Mother is here instead. Yes?

Divine Mother: Yes, correct—exactly. Ego involvement is intense for her. It will not be resolved this lifetime. She can't yet remove her own blocks as you did—and you did.

Wendy: (pause) How am I by the way?

Divine Mother: You are fine. Very, very fine. [Tumors] will be gone soon and so will the ties that bound you to her. Compassion overrules. You will seek compassion and find it in Me, my child. You will be released from this karmic load, too, because you desire it. That is why I am here for you. You love Me and you love the Father and know the choice was yours to believe the truth, no longer lies.

Wendy: Thank you. I feel much better.

It took a little time to adjust, but I could accept the truth because the choice is still hers; my mother can awaken at a future point, just not now. It was a great relief to know, and to know my efforts to help were not lost, but would take effect then. And that is when I realized the enormous benefit of having had her as my mother: it forced me to forge a path back to Divine Mother, for myself and "inadvertantly" for anyone who wants to know Her again, a path that would lead soon after this to that rendezvous in Ojai with clarity, transcendence, Reality, and the unity of All. It was not what my mother consciously set out to do, but I can't imagine anything better she could have done for me—and for you.

To reach that level of detachment, I dealt that night with the sadness of not having a mother, not in the future and not in the past. This was before Bette Eadie's book, *Embraced by the Light*, told of the existence of a life-review on the other side, but Divine Mother echoed it by interrupting my sorrow with a life-review *on this side*. We revisited the scenes of my life as I had perceived them to be: without a mother. Then She showed me the truth, and I saw She had been with me in every one. I wrote in my journal, "Divine Mother was always there, even when I couldn't see Her. I cried so much. I *did* have a real mother. And I have Her now."

A few weeks later I was suddenly laid off due to the recession. The loss of my mother, Alex's illness, the tumors, and this putting my finances and health in jeopardy because I couldn't pay the rent *and* make the insurance payments for the operation, was a shock. The shock, however, allowed for great change when a friend came that night to chant. After we finished, she said out of the blue, "I don't tell many people this, but I want to tell you. I was molested as a child."

With all my defenses dismantled, there was no stopping its rapid rise to consciousness, "I've never told a living soul about this, but I was sexually abused by my mother."

And just like that, I was free of the maternal poison that had kept me emprisoned for over 40 years—and Divine Mother could not have done it more artfully.

Backtracking through Illusion to Truth

That was the preparation. Divine Mother would now handle the actual Spiritual Process itself with me directly, beginning with this Divine Meditation on June 8, 1991. I was trying to make sense of the sexual abuse now that it had become conscious; what I could not understand at all was why it had ever happened.

>*Divine Mother*: Be at peace, child, and know that this transformation is your benefit from many hours of chanting. Please know that all is well and you are taken care of by Me and support around you, now and always. You were traumatized (very long pause) as a child of God and survived as a child of God. No harm can ever enter in from anyone at any time, no matter what the belief system dictates to be true. You were protected, you are protected. That is surely consolation.
>
>*Wendy*: Mother, *why* [did it happen]?
>
>*Divine Mother*: To become a Divine Mother in truth, light and understanding; to know that nothing harmful ever happens in truth. ... The [rocky roads] are benefit to you, no question. Please believe Me when I say so. Time will construct itself around you now, no longer the reverse. [I would control the events occurring in time; they would no longer control me.] Sexual chakra energy is transformed to higher powered meditation and consenting your will to the will of God.
>
>*Wendy*: (alarmed) Haven't I done that?
>
>*Divine Mother*: Surely you have, but remains linger to dissolve in time, precious time.
>
>*Wendy*: What am I supposed to do?
>
>*Divine Mother*: Be assured of this: you are making progress toward the goal of writing

and meditating that you desire in your heart
to give the world. Continue. Not over yet.
    Wendy: (starting to cry) It's not -
    Divine Mother: Not over yet, because
you still must release the remains of time and
you will, assuredly you will. It is hard, but not
impossible. Courage, my child, peace, and
know that you will overcome all transgres-
sions this lifetime. Now and evermore. Amen.

I did not know what Divine Mother meant by still
having to "release the remains of time," but I had been given
a clue: I never once felt like a victim of the sexual abuse; I felt
responsible. That sense of responsibility, often misinterpreted by survivors as guilt, had to have a purpose. I meditated
then to find the purpose and in that way came upon *the original cause,* the root, of the sexual abuse.

Once the Divine Meditation began, I was instantly
propelled into a past life in India thousands of years ago,
one that felt as if it had been impatiently waiting all that
time for recognition. The life was not reviewed but relived
through the consciousness I had then, impulse by unpleas-
ant sexual impulse. I was a man in the interior of something
akin to a hut, having sex with the very undelighted mother
I had then. My sexual greed came entirely from the ego and
entirely without conscience. Only my needs mattered because, to the mind I had then, only my needs existed.

The disrespect I felt for *myself* in India was so intolerable that I, as this man, projected it on to all women. That
disrespect certainly came back to me in my current lifetime:
from my father, my mother, Michel, and many men who regarded me as a sexual object. Like the symbolic meaning of
the fawn appearing early in the Divine Meditations, I had
been defenseless against the cruelty of men, but now I knew
it had been *for a reason.* I could not have defenses until I experienced first-hand the suffering that I—as a man—had
caused other women during that lifetime in India; they

had been without defenses, too.

Yet to forgive myself as that man, I needed more information from Divine Mother.

> *Divine Mother*: You are love, child. That is why I am with you always. In India, there was a time when men ruled over women as a "natural" function of divinity. There were many transgressions made at that time in the name of several gods. It was exposed to you as wrong, child, before your death. There was a hearing. Many tribulations and trials ... your trials were used with you as an example of misusing women -
>
> *Wendy*: (suck in my breath, knowing it is true)
>
> *Divine Mother*: You realized the error in all ways of abuse and chose then to take up the cause for Divine Motherhood. That's why the drive has been with you, even so have I, to enlighten the world about women, peace, love, gentleness, kindness, and non-abusive behavior in men. That is why you chose mother to abuse you, to remember these very scenes you have remembered because your guilt was very intense over this. You did not have a way to realize you could transcend guilt into truth and understanding. All the pieces fit now. You were raised in a world that demanded your betraying women, and then it changed on you and against you, forever it seemed.
>
> *Wendy* (crying, I feel so badly about what I did.)
>
> *Divine Mother*: But you *do* care about women, and it is women, it is the women's movement that draws you into evolvement at this point in time. You have much to do for

women in freeing them in all ways, especially [from the] ancient male abuse of women: *many* women now were men who abused in the past [which is why they are being abused now]. Sacred sex is encompassing love in all forms, all the senses, the Being Itself, the mind, the soul, the body—everything is used in making love.

This particular Divine Meditation, which definitely took a few days to absorb, proved to be the most important information I have ever been given. It made complete sense of my life, and produced a freedom so total it surpassed even that of the near-death. The truth and numinosity reduced the lingering effects of the past to dust and blew them away, so that only the *conscious recognition* of my eternal goodness, holiness, light and love remained.

You can see how it is a perfect exemplar of the Spritual Process outlined on pages 210-211:

The Spiritual Process in Action

1. The karmic problem was isolated as sexual abuse
2. Divine Mother located the original cause
3. Divine Mother explained it
4. I understood it
5. I realized my actions were based on illusion, thus creating the misperception that I was a terrible person
6. My feeling so bad about it and crying was deepest internal apology
7. I forgave myself in the aftermath of the meditation because I understood what happened
8. My forgiveness released the guilt
9. Only the truth of my eternal goodness, holiness, light and love remained

This was Divine Mother's answer to Her own question in the first chapter of this book when She asked me, as She asks each of us, "What if all the terrible things you ever thought about yourself weren't true?"

Such an extremely brief detour into the past, instead of innumerable lifetimes in the future, proved that none of the terrible things I thought about myself were true in this life, and none of them were true in India. I was taught falsely by the world and by myself, and I believed it, just as we have all been taught falsely by the world and by ourselves, and believed it—when the truth is that we all love women, we all love men, we all love each other and we all love ourselves. Beneath the guilt, this is the only truth there is to know. It is the Reality we share.

Realizing all of this by experiencing it internally with Divine Mother ensures for you, as it ensured for me, that even the worst can be made the best by Her. It will open the vista of a future filled with freedom and joy for anyone willing to confront their illusions *for only a few moments* in the Spiritual Process with Divine Mother.

This Divine Meditation so importantly proved, too, that the ego never suddenly materializes in anyone's life. It was manufactured in the distant past by a single misperception, a single negative cause that was only awaiting the trigger of a similar event in this life to appear. The misperception is exposed in this manner for our benefit so that we may become conscious of it by experiencing it, release it through the Spiritual Process, and in that way end any suffering.

When you engage in the Spiritual Process, you too will know that only misperception ever stood between you and goodness, between you and holiness, between you and love, between you and the light. You will understand what really happened in your life and why: a simple misperception simply caused mistaken action. The effects of misperception are only part of our everyday reality until they are consciously corrected through the Reality of the Spiritual Process or until, as Divine Mother said, all the pieces fit.

"Do unto others as you would have them do unto you," because what we do *will* be done to us—but only in an effort to awaken us to our goodness, holiness, light and love. That is justice at its most beautiful, and this is justice too: there are no victims. We have all participated in or observed the errors of the ego in ourselves or in another without consciously correctly them, and only that created our negative karma now. At one point or another, we have all sown exactly what we reap; we have just denied it.

Yet the grace of *understanding*, coupled with the forgiveness that follows it, releases every shred of the effects of negative karma, making the plan for our salvation the path we ourselves made; we just return by the way we came. The misperception of the ego, extended over that path, and over time, with the sole intent of maintaining fear to keep us from the One Mind that knows only truth, is dismantled *within moments* by Divine Mother in the Spiritual Process, revealing the Reality of our goodness, holiness, light and love, already there.

And now we are Home again—in our hearts, in our minds and in our lives, here on earth and far beyond.

20

Home Again

With liberation came stabilization. Around such a firm foundation, miracles flowed as naturally as water and have not stopped ...

... from Divine Mother telling me the date of the operation to remove the last vestige of "the remains of time," the tumors, 5 months before anyone, not even the doctor, could know the series of events that would have to fall in place for it to happen at all, to the information about the Northridge earthquake 6 months before it occurred ... or how to keep safe from negativity by putting ourselves in protective light *and making sure to ask for that light to be protected, too* ... how to subdue our environment and turn it to light ... how to manifest ... being given the content of conversations verbatim before having them ... profound and spectacular Divine Meditations with visual views of the future for all of us ... what happens when we leave here and pass over ... how the True Self absorbs the personality at the time of death and instead of becoming less, we become more ... what life is like on the other side ... how the soul transits from birth to death and back again ... other planes of existence and what we do there ... what Divine Mother is like when She is not in form ... the transcendent enlightenment that occurred so naturally in Ojai when it could not have happened without the Spiritual

Process preceding it. Even the events of my daily life have a miraculous ring, from how the gift of time has constructed itself around me, as Divine Mother said it would, to write and teach and give what I know, to one brief story that says it all:

In late 1990, a television program aired the plight of suffering Rumanian babies in such desperate need of adoption I was moved to tears and chanted with all my heart: since I could not afford to adopt one, *please,* Divine Mother, let someone do it in my place. A year later, just after the Spiritual Process had occurred, and the recession was in full swing, I worked for only a few weeks as a receptionist in a doctor's office. One day a woman came in. She too was tall and blonde, and looked so much like me that I smiled. Intrigued by the startling resemblance, I glanced at her chart: we lived only a mile apart, and her birthday was *exactly* the same as mine; day, month and year.

This was so unusual that after the woman left, I asked the nurse why she had come. "Oh, she's just getting used to her new life. She adopted a Rumanian baby last year."

Blessings with similar synchronicity occur every day, enabling me to count my blessings in facts now as an adult instead of buttons as a child. As was true for me then, I am Home again in a garden, symbolizing so perfectly how the spiritual journey truly is one without distance.

The garden grows under the sparkling California sun on land revered, as it was when I was little, by the Gabrielino Indians. The Pacific Ocean lies to the west, the Santa Monica Mountains to the north, becoming the great San Gabriel Mountains of my childhood in the east. I am complete and whole with Divine Mother again as shiny strawberries and hardy red rhubarb flourish near cream-colored roses heady with their own scent. Yellow hibiscus preen in the sunlight, crickets chirp in the shade, and luscious grapes grow green on the vine, not far from the graceful columbine.

In the harmony of color and sound, in the light and life all around, there is only the profound security of truth.

Cool breezes whisper in the late afternoon as the sun starts to set. Stars appear at twilight to greet the moon and then quietly close the day on what is, after all, the wonderful life Grandpa promised I would have, and have had for many years now with Her.

Because of Divine Mother I know what I did not consciously know in childhood: who I am, where I came from, and where I am going. I know, too, Her true identity: Divine Mother is the Original Cause of All. She is the light, and the effect of light is love—just as we, Her children, are the light, and the effect of our light is love.

In the tranquil garden whisperings are the great archtones of bliss: the presence of the Infinite, returned and released through the True Self, united and unified with All. Divine Mother's fountain of light, cascading into sparkling love—here, there and everywhere, inside and outside each one of us—is the real fountain of youth. With no worry to leave its trace, the True Self is forever young.

Looking over the earlier parts of my life in the quiet of the garden, an observer might think no card had been in my favor, and that by such slender odds no one could become self-sustaining. Yet anyone using inner sight would have seen the fountain of Divine Mother's light from the beginning and known then it could only lead to the sustenance of real love, to the fulfillment of the life Fanny Appleton did not have time to complete, a woman who, in her own words, said she had "since my earliest childhood heard God walking in the garden;" felt she did "so very, very little right," but would come to know, with "gratitude even for the past," "a right spirit within her" ... and, in this new life in a subsequent century, fulfill her heart's desire that she "never mistake the living fountain."

With eyes open to the light and love of the living fountain, with eyes opened by the light and love of the living fountain, it is possible to see clearly now how everyone had a purpose in that fulfillment, and such a simple purpose: in their own ways, each offered me the opportunity to choose again, to choose a *metabote*, a transition into newness, a resurrection into light and love, a metamorphosis into bliss and joy, just as I offered it to them.

And what do any of us do in life but offer the chance to choose again? We love one another so deeply that we are willing to come to earth in support of each other's salvation and, on a living stage of comedy and tragedy, play out the opportunities scripted by our individual karma to choose again between the contrasts prevailing over all of us: Am I light or dark? Am I day or night? Am I morning or evening? Am I love or fear? Am I really just an ego or a magnificent child of God?

In my story, as in everyone's, some chose correctly, some did not, but that is all that happened here. In the end, the whole world over, that is all that happens here. And by being here with us so we may consciously engage our mind with Hers, Divine Mother ensures the correct choice.

If you take a moment to let your mind become quiet like the garden, and repeat aloud the word "Om"—the mantra of enlightenment; the most sacred expression of spiritual knowledge in Hinduism, and the Supreme Consciousness which includes the three states of waking, dreaming and the unconscious—the sound you hear is the one first spoken most often by most children in most countries of the world:

Om...om..om.ommomomomomom—Mom.

And if you do it again, you will hear Mama.

After all you have read, and after all you now know, won't you please take another moment in the quiet to meet Her again, too?

Appendix A

A-1: Howe-Leavitt Genealogy

My maternal grandfather eleven generations ago was John Leavitt (b.1608). He married Sarah Gilman (b. 1622). Their daughter and my great-aunt ten generations earlier, Sarah Leavitt (b. 1659), married the widower Samuel Howe (b. 1642) on September 18, 1685. Samuel's son by his first marriage was David Howe.

John Leavitt was David Howe's grandfather by marriage; my great-aunt Sarah was his stepmother. Her children with Samuel Howe were David's and my blood relations, making me his tenth generation niece by marriage and a blood relation of his siblings through Sarah with John Leavitt as the mutual, direct-line ancestor.

In addition, descendants of the first *and* second Mrs. Samuel Howes intermarried, tying me genetically to all the subsequent Howes as cousins and, as unforseen as this was on my part, to the head of the Mormon Church, Brigham Young: his great-great-grandfather was Samuel Howe, and because of the intermarriages in the families, another great-great-grandfather was David Howe. Brigham Young's great-great-grandmother, David Howe's wife, and I share a common ancestor in John Paybody, creating for me another link to the Howe line.

A-2:   Howe-Leavitt-Appleton-Longfellow Genealogy

John Leavitt's son, Moses, married Dorothy Dudley, daughter of Governor Thomas Dudley; I directly descend from their union. The Howe-Leavitt-Appleton-Longfellow connections can be seen here:

1) Governor Dudley's great-granddaughter, Elizabeth, married Sam Appleton's grandson, John Appleton;

2) Governor Dudley's great-grandson, Samuel Rogers, married Appleton's daughter, Judith Appleton;

3) Governor Dudley's great-grandson, Daniel Rogers, married Appleton's granddaughter, Sarah Appleton;

4) Governor Dudley's granddaughter, Mary Woodbridge, married a subsequent Sam Appleton.

5) Samuel Appleton's granddaughter, Mary Appleton, married Nathaniel Thomas, and they are the ones who lived in Marshfield, Massachusetts, where I lived. Thomas's grandmother was the sister of my great-grandmother generations earlier, Sarah Gilman Leavitt, whose daughter Sarah (section A-1) married David Howe's father, Samuel Howe. This means that Thomas's grandmother was my direct-line great-aunt generations before and both women, of course, had the same mother from whom I directly descend, too.

It is this last marriage that directly links the Appleton-Dudley connection with the Howe-Leavitt connection, uniting all four families. Once the Howes are tied in, Longfellow follows as David Howe's relation through John Paybody, a direct ancestor of David Howe's wife and a man from whom I descend. This creates for me another tie to the Howe line (section A-1) and a link to Longfellow himself.

Appendix B

Reincarnation

While always accepted in the East, reincarnation has finally *regained* considerable acceptance in the West. Earlier, reincarnation was taught by Pythagoras in ancient Greece, and Plato said the universe would disappear without it, i.e. there would be no reason to *have* a universe; indeed, as Divine Mother notes in the section on Genesis in this book, the universe was created when we fell from Divine Consciousness and needed a way to remember it.

Further, reincarnation was openly discussed in the Gnostic Gospels, widely embraced in the West before being removed from Biblical and Christian doctrine—and before Emperor Justinian, as well as others controlling the church, mandated by law in 553 A.D. that public belief in reincarnation be forbidden. (*Harper's Encyclopedia of Mystical and Paranormal Experience*)

Still, the Bible does maintain these references to reincarnation in the New Testament:

Matthew 17:11-13

The disciples asked him, "Why then do the teachers of the law say that Elijah must come first?"

Jesus replied, "To be sure, Elijah comes and will restore all things. But, I tell you, Elijah has already come, and they did not recognize him." ... Then the disciples understood that he was talking to them about John the Baptist.

Luke 9:7-9

Now Herod the tetrarch heard about all that was going on. And he was perplexed because some were saying that John had been raised from the dead, others that Elijah had appeared, and still others that one of the prophets of long ago had come back to life.

*

A Course in Miracles never says that reincarnation does not occur, but rather, "For our purposes, it would not be helpful to take any definite stand on reincarnation." Like not taking a stand on Divine Mother, this approach was due to the reluctance to include knowledge for the student beyond the parameters of the set curriculum: "The ego will be enough for him to cope with. ... Reincarnation would not, under any circumstances, be the problem to be dealt with *now*." The italics are in the text, and deliberate; reincarnation is to be dealt with once the ego has been recognized.

A Course in Miracles also states that, "In the ultimate sense, reincarnation is impossible," because a body, past or present, is a manifestation of the ego and, "in the ultimate sense," an illusion. Just because reincarnation is defined as an illusion, however, does not meant it isn't experienced. Like the other ego manifestations of fear, grief, guilt, anger and negative karma, which are very real to us until they are dissolved by the light of Divine Mother, *we do experience reincarnation*.

As *A Course in Miracles* goes on to say, "There is always some good in any thought which strengthens the idea that life and the body are not the same." When the purpose of reincarnation is past—when we have learned from it that we are not this body but an eternally existing soul; when we have learned that the original errors of the ego are in the far distant past as we perceive it, and when we have corrected them in the present—the value of reincarnation as a teaching tool is over. Belief in it will fade with all the other illusions we once maintained and then is reincarnation, like the need for miracles, ended.

Appendix C

The Book of Job

There is very little Biblical reference to the period between the absolute presence of God and the act of genesis itself, but I believe one clearly exists in **Job 38: 4-21** when God tells us, by telling Job, that we existed prior to the beginning of the world:

Job 38:4
Where were you when I laid the earth's foundation?
    Tell me if you understand.
Who marked off its dimensions? Surely you know!
Who stretched a measuring line across it?
    On what were its footings set, or
Who laid its cornerstones—
    While the morning stars sang together
And all the angels shouted for joy?

And so it continues until God says:

Job 38:19
What is the way to the abode of light?
    And where does darkness reside?
Can you take them to their places?
    Do you know the paths to their dwellings?
<u>Surely you know for you were already born!</u>
<u>You have lived so many years!</u>

Connecting...

—To write Wendy Scott
   with questions, comments or prayer requests

—To be on the mailing list
   a) for Wendy's lectures on Divine Mother and/or
   b) for "The Divine Mother Series of Guided Divine
      Meditations"

—To have her visit your group or organization
   a) to lecture on Divine Mother, or
   b) to present "The Divine Mother Series of
      Guided Divine Meditations"

—To order audio cassette tape(s)
   a) of the book, *Meet Divine Mother*
   b) "An Introductory Guided Divine Meditation"
   c) "The Divine Mother Series of Guided Divine Med-
      itations"
   d) or request information about them

... please so indicate in your correspondence and send it to:

Wendy Scott
c/o Gold Fire Press
P. O. Box 12873
Marina del Rey, CA 90295

or log on to: www.Divinemother.net

Dates, addresses, prices, essays, stories, updates, and other kinds of information are available at the Internet address. Book and tape orders, as well as e-mail to Wendy, can be sent directly from there.